Everyday

Faith

FOR YOUR

Family

Simple rhythms to bring connection, joy, and peace into your daily routine

MARINA HOFMAN, PhD

Best-Selling Author, *Women in the Bible Small Group Bible Study*

Everyday Faith For Your Family: Simple rhythms to bring connection, joy, and peace into your daily routine
Copyright ©2025 Marina Hofman, PhD

978-1-998815-50-0 Soft Cover
978-1-998815-51-7 E-book

Published by Castle Quay Books
Little Britain, Ontario, Canada | Jupiter, Florida, USA
(416) 573-3249 | info@castlequaybooks.com | www.castlequaybooks.com

To my husband, daughter, and community of friends:
thank you for all you have contributed.
— Marina Hofman

Scripture quotations marked (NIV) are taken from the Holy Bible, New International Version®, NIV® Copyright ©1973, 1978, 1984, 2011 by Biblica, Inc.® Used by permission. All rights reserved worldwide.

Author's Note: The testimony recounted in this book reflects my personal recollection and a good-faith review of available documentation. Portions of this story have been shared previously through various media platforms, including international radio broadcasts.

This book is offered for inspirational purposes only and is not intended as a substitute for the medical advice of physicians. The reader should regularly consult a physician in matters relating to his/her health and particularly with respect to any symptoms that may require diagnosis or medical attention. Outcomes described are personal to the author and may not be typical.

Library and Archives Canada Cataloguing in Publication
Title: Everyday faith for your family : simple rhythms to bring connection, joy, and peace into your daily routine / by Dr Marina H Hofman.
Names: Hofman, Marina H., 1981- author
Identifiers: Canadiana (print) 20250311097 | Canadiana (ebook) 20250311100 | ISBN 9781998815500
   (softcover) | ISBN 9781998815517 (EPUB)
Subjects: LCSH: Families—Religious life. | LCSH: Christian life. | LCSH: Christian education of children.
Classification: LCC BV4526.3 .H64 2026 | DDC 248.4—dc23

CASTLE QUAY BOOKS

Meet Dr. Marina Hofman

Marina Hofman, PhD, is the multi-award-winning author of *Women in the Bible: Small Group Bible Study* and its companion video series. An international speaker, professor, and frequent media guest, she champions faith and family, sharing her testimony of God's redemption and healing after life-threatening trauma with audiences worldwide.

Known for her warmth, authentic voice, and deep faith in God, Marina inspires courage and hope in everyday family life through an engaging style that combines biblical scholarship with practical wisdom. A dedicated wife and homeschooling mom, she has a passionate vision to see lives transformed and experiencing the abundant life in Jesus Christ.

Learn more and read Marina's powerful testimony of God's healing and redemption at www.womeninthebible.info.

Follow Marina on YouTube (@MarinaHofman) and Instagram (@MarinaHofman), or email her at marinahofman@gmail.com.

Contents

You Are Chosen
An invitation to parents at the starting line   9

Part One: The Turning Point
When I realized something had to change

   1: The Wake-Up Call   13

Part Two: The First Steps
Weaving values into everyday rhythms

   2: The Experiment   23

Part Three: Faith-Based, Family-Centered Parenting
A values-based approach

   3: Simple Rhythms for Faith That Grows   39
   4: Simple Rhythms for a Family That Flourishes   63
   5: Simple Rhythms for a Home That Thrives   79
   6: Simple Rhythms for Connection Amid Hurry, Noise,
      and Busyness   97

Part Four: An Invitation
Choosing loving connection, joy, and peace

   7: Making Everyday Faith Yours   129

Bonus: Homeschooling by Faith
Reflections on what we've learned   145

You Are Chosen

An invitation to parents at the starting line

GOD DELIGHTS IN YOU! **God chose *you* to be a parent, entrusting you with a precious life.** This sacred calling invites you to guide and shape a soul by loving and caring for your child as God loves and cares for you.

Will you embrace this calling wholeheartedly and give your best as you raise the child God has entrusted to you?

God has chosen you for this time and purpose and will provide guidance and wisdom at every step. Lean into all God has for your family!

Raising a child who is loving, respectful, and kind is a daily labor of love. Be encouraged by the legacy you're building—children who love God and shine God's light. Even though we won't get everything right, we're shaping a way of life that helps our children know and love God.

I invite you to embrace faith-based, family-centered parenting— to nurture a home rooted in love and faith. Start where you are—one small, faithful step at a time—and may you find wisdom and encouragement here for the journey of becoming the parent God is shaping you to be.

Yours,

Marina Hofman

Part One

THE TURNING POINT

When I realized something
had to change

One

THE WAKE-UP CALL

WHEN MY DAUGHTER was a newborn, I faced a moment of truth. After I fed her, she fell asleep in my arms. I meant to simply hold her, to take her in, but before long my eyes drifted to my phone.

I don't know how long I sat there—one hand holding Willow, the other scrolling—but it was too long. Eventually, I looked down, and she was awake, quietly gazing up at me—my little angel.

The most precious gift from God looked at me with pure love while I looked away, wasting the moment on my phone. I felt awful.

To be honest, I had chosen my phone over my newborn. I could offer excuses, but it was mindless scrolling. Why? A reflex to reach for my phone. A drive to multitask. The ease of zoning out instead of embracing quiet. I had no idea how deeply I would long for those sacred newborn moments years later.

Right then, I chose presence—two hands for my child, not one for her and one for my phone. **That quiet wake-up call became a turning point**—not just in parenting, but in life.

A Life-and-Death Moment

As I sat waiting for the ambulance on a bitterly cold day, I felt my life was over. It wasn't, but I knew something was terribly wrong: I couldn't speak, I wasn't sure who I was, didn't know whether my husband was alive, and my body throbbed with intense pain. Just when life was going well—newly married, with an exciting job offer—my world crashed down.

My husband and I were driving home from a long weekend getaway when a driver in the oncoming lane dropped his head. In a split second, his vehicle veered into our lane at full speed. There was nowhere to turn: the highway was under construction, and we were on a bridge with guardrails. In that moment, I believed I was about to die.

My husband maneuvered so we wouldn't hit anyone else; we absorbed the full impact. As the brakes failed, he reached over, pressed my head against the headrest, and leaned across me so his body absorbed the airbags' force—an act that saved my life.

I suffered four lacerations in my bowels; the surgeon said I was nearly dead when I arrived at the hospital. No one could explain how I survived.

I had been given a gift—the experience of God's power to breathe life into death. I realized life is fleeting—and **I resolved to embrace every moment more fully.**

I faced a long road of recovery before learning to live fully. I had severe amnesia. My executive function was severely damaged—I had to relearn English, daily tasks, and self-care. I was traumatized and developed anxiety, depression, and severe PTSD. My body quivered most of the day; simple things triggered panic. Emotionally, I lived under a dark cloud.

We all face seasons of struggle, trauma, and great trials with those we love most. How do we survive the hardest days and emerge better people?

God began to turn the pain and loss into purpose. I share this because it gives me hope: **God is able to transform our lives—to take our brokenness and restlessness and bring healing, renewal, and wholeness.** I needed this reminder years later when I looked at my life and saw hurry, noise, busyness, and distraction—and realized I was choosing them, even with the gift of a child in my arms. I longed for another reset—and I knew I could choose presence over distraction by leaning into God.[1]

The Miracle

God can do more than we can ask or imagine. I have lived this. My "more than I could ask or imagine" was a simple prayer for strength to handle basic self-care.

God's plan for my life far exceeded my prayer. I wanted to survive. God wanted me to experience a deeper awareness of the presence of the Holy Spirit, the power of the risen Christ, and the faithfulness of a loving God.

Healing was slow. After two years of therapy, I was still in rough shape, and I feared I might never get pregnant. The doctor confirmed there was almost no chance of conceiving because of internal injuries and scar tissue. I doubted whether I should even try to have a child because I was so emotionally fragile.

But in time, I became pregnant—a miracle beyond my comprehension. I felt deeply loved by God. While pregnant, I experienced near-complete healing of the scar tissue as my organs shifted. My emotional recovery leapt forward. Truly, more than I could have imagined.

Willow's birth fulfilled a lifelong dream, and I was determined to be the best mom I could be.

---

1. Explore more of Marina's miracle-filled journey at WomenInTheBible.info for the worldwide *Unshackled!* dramatization (available in eighteen languages) and other major outlets, including Family Radio.

Turning Down the Noise

I researched and tried to follow every piece of advice on caring for a newborn. There were so many things I should do and so many I shouldn't that I was in constant uncertainty.

At one point, I was told by a doctor to wake the newborn every two hours during the night—turn on all the lights, make banging noises, and place a cold can against her skin. It sounded insane, but, against my instincts, I set my alarm and fed Willow with all the lights on, though I skipped the banging noises and the cold can. After a few days, I was exhausted—I broke down and told my nurse friend everything. She calculated that the baby was gaining weight at a very healthy pace—I could stop.

At our next doctor's visit, I was told to sit and leave Willow on the examination table, alone. The doctor was not standing beside my baby and did not seem very attentive. I nervously asked, "Is the baby okay there? She can roll over." She laughed—"No, honey, babies don't roll over at this age," her back still to my baby. Hesitantly, I mumbled, "Well, Willow can." A moment later, Willow whipped her arm over and started to roll toward the edge of the table. Thank God I caught her.

I felt deep frustration at being dismissed and belittled in my role as a mother. Those appointments left me disarmed. I thought I had to do as I was told, and I questioned whether I truly knew what was best for my daughter.

We parents need to forgive ourselves, and first-time parents need extra grace. It's not easy when an authority figure questions our parental instincts. I wish someone had told me that it's okay to question, to speak up, and to trust my gut even when others don't.

These early weeks helped me realize that something had to change. **I needed to turn down outside voices, stop chasing what "everyone else" was doing—and lean into God's leading.**

I was willing to try. And so began an experiment—a whole new way of parenting and living. I'd like to share with you how I broke with social norms to raise a child who loves Jesus and others—and how you can live out faith-based, family-centered values as you lead your family.

Are you ready to cultivate loving connection, joy, and peace in your family? Start here—with a few reflections to guide your first steps.

Reflection

1. How has God turned pain, loss, or hardship in your past into growth or new purpose for drawing close to Him?

_____

_____

_____

_____

_____

2. Do you believe God can do more than you can ask or imagine in your life and family? What is your "ask or imagine" for yourself and your family?

_____

_____

_____

_____

_____

3. Is there an area where you're following other voices instead of your God-given instincts? What's a value-aligned alternative you can try this week?

Family Conversation Starters

- "I'm reading a new book that talks about the importance of faith and trusting God. What does faith mean to you?"
- "What's one way you see God's everyday miracles—big or small—in our family?"
- "This book also talks about being more present and less distracted. How do you feel about me making an effort to spend more quality time with you?"

Rhythms for This Week

1. Write down ways God has been faithful in your life and family. Let this build your trust that God will continue to be faithful and bring good to your family.

2. Memorize and post this Scripture where you will see it every day to encourage you on the journey to lead well: "God is able to do immeasurably more than all we ask or imagine" (Ephesians 3:20).

3. Schedule a time to pause and pray. Tell God about your struggles and when you followed other voices rather than leaning into God's leading. Ask God for the courage and strength to trust Him—and to take this journey to lead your family well.

Part Two

THE FIRST STEPS

Weaving values into everyday rhythms

Two

THE EXPERIMENT

AFTER THE TRAUMA of our car crash and the injuries that followed, how could I possibly be a good mom? Those early negative experiences showed me I was following other voices instead of trusting the instincts God gave me.

I chose a new path: to listen to my God-given instincts and realign our family life around faith-based, family-centered values.

The questions that follow grew out of conversations with parents. Each segment stands alone—perfect for a quick moment.

I share simple, everyday rhythms that nurtured our family's connection, joy, and peace—what worked for us—so you can adapt them at home and on the go.

In these brief moments we share, may you be encouraged and empowered to bring your best and see God at work in your life and family on the beautiful yet sometimes messy journey of parenting— as you take the simple steps toward faith-filled, values-based everyday rhythms.

What's driving the crisis families face today?

Are you concerned about the dynamics that many families are struggling with? Kids are on endless screens, eating meals alone, and feeling isolated in their bedrooms. There are so many broken homes. Parents feel shut out of their children's inner worlds. We see rising anxiety, addictions, and hopelessness.

Our youth are in crisis, and this crisis increasingly reaches young children. Schools are failing too many children—the number of students without minimum proficiency in reading, writing, and math is alarming. Children are hurting and angry; many feel hopeless.

I meet discouraged parents. "I have no idea what my kids do all night in their bedrooms," they tell me. They don't like what their kids are involved in, but don't know how—or whether—they have the right to correct behaviors that all their children's friends engage in.

Children of all ages show disrespect and even contempt for their parents. Culture conveys that parents are uninformed and out of touch. Children's TV programming teaches this. Advertisements feature motifs of a "dud" dad and a clueless mom. The school system, in many cases, confirms this narrative by assigning convoluted homework that teaches basic concepts in ways unfamiliar to adults. Many parents struggle to understand the new ways math is taught, even in grades 2 and 3, leaving them feeling undermined and lacking confidence.

It broke my heart recently to hear a parent share that her son was crying because he didn't understand his math lessons and couldn't do his homework. She wanted to help but couldn't figure it out either.

What's the impact? Children begin to question whether their parents can be trusted. If Dad and Mom can't decode grade-school math, can they be trusted on weightier matters?

As parents, how many times do we endure culture's condescension before we start to doubt ourselves? When do we begin to fear that our homes mirror ads where kids know it all and parents are clueless?

How often does Hollywood portray strong parent-child bonds—children treasured within healthy families? I rarely see the closeness I want for my own family modeled, so I feel like an outlier.

I don't want this world for Willow or our family. I don't want my daughter hooked on electronics, growing antisocial, or drifting away from curiosity and critical thinking. I don't want Willow to ever lose her sense of wonder and quirkiness.

I certainly don't want to feel disconnected from my child or anxious because I don't know what she's doing or who she's talking to.

Many of us need a new path—one that creates new rhythms of connection, joy, and peace.

What was the moment everything changed?

My world changed dramatically when the initial lockdown began in March 2020. I isolated at home to "flatten the curve." By day four, I was stir-crazy.

Although somewhat introverted, I started to fall apart—I missed my friends. Something felt very wrong. It prompted me to think deeply about what—and who—in my life mattered most.

My actions and heart felt out of sync.

Then close friends asked to visit, and this shocked me. I asked why they would want to be with my family in light of the COVID-19 threat.

They said they weren't afraid and that, whatever happened, they would keep living their lives. I was stunned.

Sometimes we experience a watershed moment—we witness someone living counterculturally, and it prompts us to question our assumptions. The natural response to my friend was to welcome her; we're close friends. So why did I feel a tremendous pressure to say no?

I wondered how many parts of my life reflected what I was told to do rather than what I truly believed and valued. Had I unknowingly outsourced my judgment to "what everyone's doing"?

In that moment, what did I value more—conformity to lockdown restrictions or time spent with my dear friends? I wasn't sure; I felt unable to articulate my most deeply held values.

I grew up in a Christian home and have always had a strong faith, so this inability surprised and disappointed me. I now see God's grace in the situation, because it sent me searching.

If we believe that God guides our thoughts and that there is a time for everything, then I had no reason to feel guilty. I did, however, need to reflect—to identify what I valued most and align my actions accordingly.

That moment woke me up—and sent me searching for a better way.

What happened when your actions clashed with your values?

I felt deeply unsettled as I realized a disconnect between my values and my choices. Lockdowns were tough. I was unhappy. It felt like chaos was raging, and my family was in the middle of it.

By God's grace, I realized this disconnect early, when Willow was still a young baby.

I saw the same tension everywhere: families in chaos despite their strong values. Something had to change. Something significant—matching the scale of the crisis of faith and family I saw.

If I rejected prevailing social norms, I would need to raise Willow by a countercultural standard—a "revolutionary" set of values. I would need to establish new rhythms and habits. But how?

Could I do this without looking to everyone around me or googling tips? **Could I embrace who God created my daughter to be, instead of letting her conform to the crowd?**

I decided to run an experiment for a season. **My experiment was to focus on the values I wanted to instill in my child, muster the courage to live according to those values myself, and then align our family around those values.**

I would raise Willow by our values—not cultural norms—and see whether loving connection, joy, and peace grew at home through everyday rhythms and small, simple steps of change.

How did you turn frustration into change?

I took a hard look at my life.

What was I doing—and why? How did I feel about each area of my life and our family? What did I want for myself? What did I want for my family?

The reflection was unsettling.

I realized my daily habits and choices didn't align with the life I desired. I spent more time on social media than I would want Willow to spend, and my days lacked the activities I wanted for her—the arts, nature, music, and dance. I wanted Willow to be happy and have wonderful family memories, but how often was I happy? How often did I laugh?

It seemed impossible for Willow to have a positive childhood if I didn't model the joy, peace, and zest for living I wanted for her.

The gap between where I was and where I wanted to be felt insurmountable.

I decided—at least for a season—to quiet the noise and deeply reflect on what I wanted. The result was a resolve to lead our family according to our deeply held values, regardless of the cost.

It was an arduous, lengthy process that forged a clear determination to live by our values—however countercultural—even if people thought us strange or if some friends drifted away.

What were your first steps toward a new way of parenting?

First, I acknowledged that letting other voices override my instincts wasn't working. One thing was clear: to help my child avoid the crisis overtaking many young people, I had to break from cultural norms that didn't align with my values. I needed a radically different path—with new patterns and routines.

Second, I asked God where to begin. After weeks of deep, honest reflection and prayer on what truly mattered most and the values I wanted to live by, I then shifted my focus to defining the values I wanted for our family.

Third, I wrote out my list of values—that list became a concrete starting point. It may sound basic, but I spent two months deeply reflecting on what mattered most to me. I asked myself hard questions to get to this point. I wrote the values down so I could see them clearly and return to them when I felt uncertain or faced hard decisions.

Which core values became your compass?

I narrowed my values to keep life simple and manageable: God first; my family second; health and wholeness on every level—spiritual, emotional, physical, physiological—third. These are the values I choose to live by; they form the foundation of my well-being. They are the same values I want for my husband and daughter. Everything else flows from these values.

How did change begin in your family?

Once I felt sure about my top values, I shared the journey with my husband. I needed his full buy-in to make meaningful changes to our daily family life. He readily agreed that faith, family, and health were primary for us and encouraged me to prioritize them in new ways.

Next, I considered how to make positive changes. The first step was me. **I had to lead myself with excellence before I could lead anyone else.**

I needed to admit that my daily routine included these values, but didn't revolve around them.

Could I commit to living by these values wholeheartedly? Was I willing to make a few dramatic changes in my life?

A personal commitment to my values was essential. I needed to start with myself, living by my own standards, before I could expect them of my family.

How did you begin leading yourself in a new way?

At first, leading myself felt impossible—like I was failing at every turn.

We are human, and change takes time. We have to give ourselves grace to grow and develop, forgiveness when we fall short, and the understanding that becoming our best is a lifelong journey. It's more important to focus on our daily effort than to fixate on overall successes or failures.

I found joy and encouragement in knowing that my family could take this journey together to be our best. It would bond us in positive ways.

I made a greater effort to put God first in my life. Did I struggle? Yes. I committed those struggles to God in prayer, turned to God for guidance, and chose to trust God to help me.

What about my family? Did I harbor hard feelings or resentment toward my husband? I had to let them go. Did the frustrations and demands of motherhood make me angry? I had to surrender those feelings to God in exchange for love, kindness, patience, and gentleness.

With the responsibilities of being a wife and mother and an endless list of tasks weighing on me, how could I prioritize my health? I had to find a way. There was no use burning out and getting sick. For me, that meant small, steady choices—exercising with Willow, eating better, and getting enough sleep.

There it was.

I committed to loving God first and foremost, valuing my family second, and caring for my overall well-being third. As I improved my health, I felt stronger and more able to move forward from a place of greater wholeness. Caring for myself strengthened my care for my family and increased my awareness of how my actions affected them.

Over time, living according to values became easier and more natural—day by day, one small rhythm at a time.

What shifted in your parenting as your values became clear?

To be fully committed to faith-based, family-centered parenting a significant shift in my thinking was required. In practice, this meant weighing all the advice I was given—from family, friends, and authority figures, and the cultural norms around me—without following something simply because it was popular.

We chose what we let in and released the rest—advice we could act on, and trends or "expert" tips we could kindly decline.

Instead of looking to others for models to copy, I asked: Do the habits and customs around us align with our values? If not, we chose differently.

That single question became our daily filter for decisions—big and small.

How did you communicate a new way of living to your child?

Communicating my deeply held values to my daughter was intimidating. How could I teach her to value faith above all else in the ordinary moments of our day? How could I teach her to value family? How could I guide Willow to value health and wholeness—joyfully? I chose a simple approach: learn to live out my values first, then explain them.

It became clear that my example would convey our values best. It required sacrifice. I had to surrender lesser things to choose what was most important. There was a sense of starting over. I knew that many aspects of my life and habits needed to change. I reset our rhythms to put faith, family, and health at the center.

In short, communicating my values began with my example. As I developed a new way of thinking and living, my daughter observed the change in me, and from there, I could explain why I was choosing to live counterculturally. I lived it; then I named it for her.

Simple phrases could be woven into our daily conversations—"Let's pray about this; we need God's guidance," "Family time matters because we love each other and want to stay close," and "We care for our bodies because they are a gift from God."

Over time, the "why" behind our habits became her own—and new rhythms of everyday life formed.

What flowed from your new faith-based, family-centered approach?

Leading our home with a values-based approach brought greater peace and simplified decision-making. It was working, and I wondered what would happen if I went all in.

It felt revolutionary—so different from the culture and examples around me. I began to live by our values. I stopped looking to everyone around me for a pattern to follow, stopped googling tips online, and stopped aiming for Willow to be like other kids.

We chose to love God first, value family next, and care for our health as best we could. As we succeeded in teaching Willow to care for herself, we turned our attention to caring for others and grew more aware of how our actions affected those around us.

I created a simple, repeatable framework to guide parenting decisions and discern what was best for our family. I discovered that it was empowering—it gave me a clear standard to refer to for us, a shared standard we could point to when choices felt hard.

With that framework in place, decisions became simpler, and our home grew more peaceful as our everyday rhythms bore fruit.

How do you keep rules simple—and rooted in values?

I find it's easier to establish a few clear principles than to manage endless case-by-case rules.

For example, when a friend suggests a TV show that I don't want Willow to watch, I respond, "No, thank you—our family doesn't watch that show." This communicates that our decision isn't situational—it's rooted in our values. It also feels easier than turning to Willow and saying, "No, I don't want you to watch that."

I can defer to our fundamental values rather than sounding bossy. This works for our family. Willow begins to understand why I say no to some of her requests, and she learns to evaluate what's right and best for herself. It wasn't long before I overheard her sharing our values with friends—"No, we don't watch that show because it doesn't share our family values." It made me smile to hear a little three-year-old talking about family values.

This approach also works with the children who visit our home. I can say to others, "We don't watch that show in our home," rather than "No, Willow is not allowed to watch that." The children rarely argue with me. They usually accept it as fact. When they ask why, it's an opportunity to talk about our values with them.

When I used to respond that I didn't want Willow to do something, I found that other parents would argue with me and try to convince me that it was fine. Now, when I ground my response in our family values, the opposite happens—parents often say, "Oh, we aren't going to watch that either," and then give their children a look that ends the discussion.

It's striking to see the difference in reactions. It gives us a shared, higher standard to appeal to rather than sounding bossy or overly strict. It earns the respect of other parents and makes decisions clearer, conversations calmer, and everyday moments easier to manage.

What is your vision for parenting now?

My vision is for Willow to know God deeply, be a leader among her peers, and influence her world for good. I want her identity and confidence to be rooted in Christ, with faith and God's Word serving as an anchor for her life.

I want Willow to highly value family. What is ultimately most important in life? For us, it's faith and family. My concern was how to do this in a culture that seems to resist and even to undermine both.

As for our family, I want us to be truly close. My husband is my best friend, and I hope that when Willow is older, she will be a best friend too. To get there, we are building those dynamics now—listening, supporting, laughing, and sometimes crying together—forgiving and accepting each other as God created us to be. Because I homeschool, Willow and I are together all day, every day, so we work to guard against hard feelings and choose to have hard conversations.

Willow is learning to show me respect and obedience, and in our home loving-kindness lives alongside loving authority. Authority provides the guardrails; friendship keeps our hearts connected.

At least I can share with you that I had these lofty ideals—I wanted peace, I wanted closeness, I wanted a home where we were loving and kind to each other. As we all grew closer to God and to each other—and as joy and peace deepened in our home—I knew we were on the right track.

Reflection

1. Reflect on your values. Name the three or four values you hold dearest. Which daily rhythms reflect these values—and which undermine them?

2. What personal change can you make to better align your life with your values? Commit to one change to lead your family well.

3. Do you feel caught between being present for your family and the pressures of work and home? What makes being present hard?

4. What creates distractions, hurry, and noise in your daily routines? List what you could surrender—for a season—to

make space to spend more time with your family. Reflect on the rewards of being more present in your family.

_____

_____

_____

_____

5. Who will support positive changes in your home—cheer you on and hold you accountable? Set up a time to share with them why you feel change is needed and what it might look like.

_____

_____

_____

_____

Family Conversation Starters

- "What do we want our home to feel like? What choices make our home feel that way?"
- "What gets in the way of loving connection, joy, and peace between us?"
- "What could we eliminate, and what habits could we build to increase our connection, joy, and peace ?"

Rhythms for This Week

1. Reflect on your core values and put them in writing somewhere visible.

_____

_____

_____

2. Read the lists you created—what you can surrender; what creates distractions, hurry, and noise in your daily routines; and the rewards of being present with your family. Commit these to prayer and come back to them as you progress through this book.

3. Try one step forward to lead by example this week: schedule a time (ten minutes, one hour) every day to put devices away and give your family undivided attention. See what happens!

4. Notice where connection, joy, and peace grow as you take this step forward to be more present.

Part Three

FAITH-BASED, FAMILY-CENTERED PARENTING

A values-based approach

Three

SIMPLE RHYTHMS FOR FAITH THAT GROWS

I'VE SHARED MY vision for values-based parenting with you. Here, I show how faith takes shape in everyday life.

To prioritize faith means always seeking ways to weave faith into our daily rhythms. My approach evolves as Willow grows and our daily routines change. Adapting to different seasons of life is necessary, while we strive to maintain the foundations of our faith.

In what follows, you'll find simple everyday rhythms that quietly reshape moments and days—practices you can start tonight and carry into tomorrow. Creating a new way of living begins with small changes—allowing ordinary family moments to become sacred.

As you read these chapters, I hope you'll highlight what stands out, and begin to help your family grow in loving connection, joy, and peace by cultivating one small rhythm at a time.

When you're ready, return to your highlights and take the next small, faithful step in leading your family.

What is the foundational practice of faith?

Prayer is an integral part of my spiritual life and our family's daily faith practices—the core of our faith journey. Prayer keeps us grateful, trusting in God, and centered on God. Prayer belongs in every part of daily life.

It's not enough to pray only before we eat. We need to start and end the day with prayer—and stay mindful of prayer throughout the day.

Now, I can imagine how this sounds to some readers! I was far from praying throughout the day with Willow when I began my journey.

So my husband and I committed to praying out loud together every morning with Willow present. This was easy since she was a baby when we started. By the time she was a toddler, it was a daily routine, and her participation was natural. If she slipped away while we prayed, I explained the importance of our family prayer time, and I gently shared how I felt when she left—that I missed her and loved to hear her pray, hoping it would prompt her not to sneak off next time.

I don't want to force what I hope will come from her heart, yet I do want to guide her with gentle expectations and practice during our prayer times. When she feels unsure about what to say, my husband and I offer words she can use or make her own. On difficult days when she was little, we let her eat a snack, keep coloring, or even practice her handstands while we prayed. My goal was to help her form a lifelong habit of prayer while keeping this sacred time a positive experience for her.

As she gets older, other priorities can creep up just when we are about to pray. I still remind her of the importance of this family time and emphasize the value of committing our needs and wants to God, telling God our concerns, and asking for God's protection over all we do. Ultimately, it's okay to insist on her presence during our family prayer time. I teach her to form other habits—sitting at the table while we eat, keeping her bedroom door open while friends are over, making her bed every morning—so why not include prayer time in our schedule and stick to it? It's one of our most important rhythms for a family faith that grows.

Prayer is the foundation of my personal faith. Over the years, I've nurtured the habit of praying throughout the day when I am alone or engaged in simple tasks—getting ready in the morning, trying to fall asleep at night, gardening, cleaning, and tackling household projects like painting. I pray while exercising and driving—long drives are wonderful times to pray and listen to God. Whenever an anxious thought or fear enters my mind, I pray—even if only for a moment. When I think of the needs of family and friends, I offer up a prayer right then. I pray with the lyrics of worship songs and the words of Scripture.

The rhythm of continual prayer keeps me connected to God and my heart at peace. It builds confidence as I commit my requests to God, knowing that God hears, answers, and provides. Prayer is my lifeline.

We can all start simply and stay consistent. Pray together every day to build a rhythm of prayer. In doing so, we create space for God to transform our hearts and give us a desire to pray, making it a natural part of our daily lives.

How can we build a daily rhythm of prayer at home?

In our family, we pray aloud together in the morning after coffee—before we go our separate ways. This gives us an opportunity to start the day with thankfulness, commit our day and plans to God, ask for God's guidance in how we spend our time, pray for God's protection over our home, lift up family and friends, and pray beyond ourselves for our community, church, country, and world.

We pray a simple prayer together before meals, and at Willow's prompting, we now end with the Lord's Prayer.

Our nightly prayer time is the most consistently meaningful part of my day as a mom. It's just Willow and me when she climbs into bed. I always ask her what she'd like to pray about. When she was little, she often wanted something impossible, like asking God to make unicorns real. Even now, she has big prayer requests, and I'm reminded that God has made her a visionary and a dreamer.

Often, she shares something that's bothering her. Or she confesses something she's done and feels unsure about. These windows into her thoughts are special opportunities for us to talk about what matters to her.

Then I pray for Willow. Praying out loud for her lets me share my heart. It's a sacred time to affirm her by thanking God for all her wonderful qualities and the kind things she's done that day. I know she pays attention even when she squirms or looks bored. I remember when she was little, I'd hear her tell others, "My mom always says I'm her angel and I am a gift from God." It was true! I reaffirmed that every night in prayer. As she grows older, it's as important as ever to affirm her and thank God for who she is and the lovely person she's becoming with God's help.

I confess that when I began praying for Willow, I didn't know what to say. I sensed the Lord leading me to these words, which I share with you in hopes they will help you when words are hard to find:

> "The LORD bless you and keep you;
> the LORD make his face to shine on you
> and be gracious to you;
> the LORD turn his face toward you and give you peace."
> (Numbers 6:24–26)

What does praying with children teach us?

Developing a prayer life with Willow has taught me so much about my daughter. How sweet were those early days when she first asked to pray! Her little prayers revealed the most significant concerns and sources of happiness in her life. She'd list all her stuffed animals by name in thanks to God. Then she gradually added requests, like asking God for Mom to give her ice cream and telling God she wanted a horse.

I was unsure how to respond when her requests expanded to a whole farm—animals and all—and I watched her grow frustrated with God as that prayer seemed unanswered. As a result of what her prayers revealed to me, we began to visit the local wildlife sanctuary regularly, which provided a reasonable alternative to becoming a farmer.

There are times when Willow prays with great dedication. She prayed for years to hear God speak to her. I admit I was deeply troubled that God didn't seem to answer her prayer. Willow outright asked me, "Why doesn't God speak to me?" I didn't know why. I wondered if God was allowing her to wait so that, when God did speak, the moment would be sacred and cherished—cherished in a way only possible when we desire something for a long time.

Indeed, that time came when she was six years old. God spoke to her heart and warned her against saying something to a friend. She told me that she really wanted to say it, but something told her not to share it. Wow. I told her, "That's the Lord!" I was excited, but she remained solemn and deep in thought. Over time, she began to recognize that "voice" of direction and assurance in other situations.

I can now point to many instances when we prayed for something together, and in time, God answered. Through daily prayer, I learn her desires. Praying together gives us both a window into each other's hearts—and through waiting, we learn to trust God's timing.

How do answered prayers shape our children—and us?

We moved to a new community days after the lockdowns began in 2020. Willow had no friends, which upset her. She decided to pray every day for God to give her a neighbor her age who could be a friend. We prayed every time we walked through our neighborhood.

It wasn't too long before we discovered that our neighbor two doors down had a grandchild, a year or so older than Willow.

To everyone's delight, Willow was convinced that the girl was an answer to our prayers, and the two bonded immediately. It turned out that the neighbor's values were much like ours. It truly seemed like a friendship from Heaven.

I often reflected that Willow's delight and wonder upon meeting our neighbor's grandchild grew out of committing this need to God in prayer. I admit that my perspective on God was challenged. I envisioned God as One who focused on *adult* things, about *serious* requests, about the problems that I couldn't solve myself. I began to see God as One who cared about everything—even Willow's small needs and her concerns about her stuffed animals. While I had internally rolled my eyes at Willow's prayers for toys, valuing them only as practice for "more important" requests, I came to realize that everything Willow prayed for mattered to God—simply because it mattered to Willow.

Our new neighborhood friend became a great blessing and presence in our lives. Truly, God answered Willow's prayer far beyond my imagination. It seemed like a special friendship that God gave to Willow because God loved her and was drawing near her. I was amazed to discover that my daughter had a connection with the great God of the universe.

It gave new meaning to my view of the little things in Willow's world. I learned to value her concerns and thoughts about things I had once dismissed as trivial. Realizing that the tiny details in Willow's life were important to God helped me care about them too—and by extension, to care more deeply about Willow.

It's transformative to see the full humanity of our child—to realize that our child is not a task to manage, but a complex human whose feelings matter, and who wants to be heard and seen. That realization changed me. I wanted to see Willow as God saw her; I wanted to care about whatever mattered to her, and I wanted to know her opinions on everything.

How do we cultivate God's presence?

We try to abide in God's presence. What does this mean? It means that, throughout the day at home, at work, and everywhere in between, we try to be the same person as we are during family prayer—kind, thoughtful, attentive, and mindful of God.

It's not easy to maintain mindfulness of God, to stay attentive to Him, especially during busy times or when our emotions flare up in frustration, anger, disappointment, or fear. Those are the moments when I struggle to be a person who embodies the fruits of the Spirit— love, joy, peace, patience, kindness, goodness, faithfulness, gentleness, and self-control.

How do we fill our lives with God's presence and peace? Listening to faith-filled music rooted in Scripture is very helpful. We play worship music or Christian radio throughout the day. We have art on our walls that turns our thoughts toward God and showcases the beauty of creation. We choose wholesome entertainment in the evening.

I believe the atmosphere of our home is shaped by what we watch and listen to. Even the books on our shelves and the toys we keep can carry an influence. For example, we don't keep anything associated with witchcraft in our home. I encourage you—if you have a "bad feeling" about an object in your home, pray about it—and consider removing it.

Fill your home and heart with what lifts your spirit—and remove anything that steals your peace.

What role does faith play when life hurts?

Faith is crucial during times of change, trauma, illness, disappointment, and every hardship we face. When I was walking through the valley of the shadow of death after our car crash, God's presence was nearer and stronger than I had ever experienced. I know God held me together.

We want to grow strong in faith before trials come, so we can stand firm when they do. We want our children to lean on their faith as an anchor for life.

With children, we can begin by responding to their seemingly small problems with a faith perspective. We pray about anything and everything important to our children—even "trivial" moments become opportunities to practice faith. Praying together also acknowledges that we see what upsets our child and that we understand their needs and want to help.

Faith is so much more than prayer, of course. During our time together before bed, we can discuss any questions or concerns our children may have. Willow often asks about Heaven at night. It's a sacred, safe time. She can tell me anything, and I won't judge her. I talk about the consequences of her actions, but I won't punish her for anything she confesses.

For example, the other night she shared something with me—the full story of an incident with a friend. She knows my perspective, so we didn't talk about it much. I told her I love her, appreciate her honesty, value our closeness, and want to trust her completely. I asked her to be completely honest with me because she can trust me with the truth. It was a peaceful and loving conversation. She responded well because she has learned that this time is sacred—a genuinely safe time and place for honest conversation. It took years to develop this level of trust.

Sometimes I raise things that happened during the day that I find unacceptable. I tell her if I feel she showed disrespect or hurt some-one's feelings, and we'll talk about why it was wrong and how she can respond differently next time. I love being able to address my concerns at a time when I am relaxed, listening, and at peace.

In this way, our faith is lived as we joyfully model its core tenets—grace, forgiveness, and compassion. We can show our child that we, too, rely on God, even when we are uncertain or afraid, or when things aren't going our way; we trust God to guide our lives. We talk about what it looks like to show God's love to others when we're hurt or upset.

Little by little, these moments form everyday rhythms of the heart. Life's challenges and struggles are transformed into opportunities to practice our faith.

What are "faith talks"—and how do we start them with kids?

Faith talks are moments when we talk about what's going on around us from a faith-based, biblical perspective. They're natural conversations—in the car, at the table, on a walk. They help children develop critical thinking and build a rhythm of sharing their experiences with us. They give us opportunities to teach our children about God and biblical principles, and to show them how to apply them to real-life situations.

From a young age, children can absorb spiritual truths. Children can understand concepts about God in meaningful ways. When Willow was about three, we watched *Beauty and the Beast* together. As the closing credits rolled, Willow commented that she loved the movie because she liked how the Holy Spirit changed the heart of the beast. I was moved—and realized the depth at which a young child can connect spiritual truths to daily life.

We can help our children grow in their understanding of spiritual matters by asking questions and sharing our own spiritual reflections with them. Faith talks can be short and honest—ask a question, listen well, and let Scripture guide the next step. Questions can be simple: "What happened? What do you think God is saying? What does the Bible say? What could we do next?" **Even one meaningful question each day around the dinner table—"Where did you see God today?"— can help our children nurture discernment.**

As children enter their teen years, faith talks help them think deeply about what it means to follow God. We can include our teens in our family decision-making. Do they feel a given activity would honor God? Why or how? We can prompt them to analyze their actions and words in the light of their faith. When they feel something is "wrong" or they don't feel comfortable, we can help them figure out what is bothering them and how God is helping them develop discernment. If God has alerted them, God will also help them know how best to respond.

As teens enter into new types of relationships, we certainly want to talk about what honors God and God's plan for their lives. Discussing how faith integrates into our lives gives our children the tools to think critically and to know what is right. When there are topics and questions that we are still trying to figure out, we can be honest. We can let our children see that our faith journey is lifelong, and sometimes we learn most when we are struggling and must press in to hear from God.

How does faith anchor older kids when life gets loud?

Faith helps older children through their struggles—I know this from my own experience. God's comfort and peace can transfer us from lives filled with anxiety, uncertainty, fear, and self-doubt into lives of lasting peace and assurance. This transformation brings confidence that our future is in God's hands, the courage to move forward despite fear, and a trust in God that outweighs our limitations.

One of the most significant challenges facing youth is a crisis of identity. They are bombarded with negative messaging and constantly driven to compare themselves to others, which creates feelings of inadequacy, emptiness, and confusion. Social media amplifies this, as youth not only compare themselves to peers but also to carefully curated images of influencers.

So how does faith in God help youth in crisis? Youth are freed from the pressures of comparison when they anchor their identity in who God created them to be. They find validation in God, rather than in the number of followers or likes they receive. They give their anxieties and insecurities to God and receive peace as they learn to trust God more deeply.

Faith empowers young people to connect with God and build authentic relationships. It shapes their values toward godly traits they can develop with God's help—to be loving, kind, and self-controlled—rather than chasing the world's shifting, often unattainable standards.

A right identity in God is based on God's truth, love, and purpose. It assures youth that they are enough when they simply embrace the beloved person God created them to be. They are deeply loved by a God who cares about them and will never abandon them. When our young people root their identity in God, comparison loses its power and hold.

These are some of the reasons we seek to build everyday rhythms of faith in our family.

How do we guide teens toward a daily, living faith?

We can encourage them to read Scripture daily, to add a verse-a-day app notification on their device, and to dig into a youth devotional. We can invite them to join us in a daily family prayer time and commit their concerns to God together. We can seek out a healthy church youth group that connects them with positive influences and biblical teaching. We can play Christian music and choose faith-based entertainment options.

We can show interest by asking their perspective on a daily Scripture verse or what they liked best about a devotional. We can ask them each morning or night how we can pray for them. At dinnertime, we can share what we are grateful for and how God was present in our day. After church services, we can ask what they thought of the service, what aspects of the sermon stood out to them, and whether they had any meaningful conversations.

You might not get much of a response, but asking shows that you care. Share your answers. Talk about what impacted you. Be real about your prayer requests.

Praying together lets us share our requests—for example, I'll ask for prayer for an upcoming appointment or meeting and admit when I feel nervous and need God's peace. I often ask Willow to pray for me. When she went through a stage of not wanting to pray out loud, I'd say, "Okay, I'll pray, but please join me and pray for me in your heart."

This helps normalize prayer and faith. Years later, I can see how those early moments shaped her. When I ask her to pray with me now, she will—or respond, "Why don't you pray—and yes, I will pray with you in my heart." She gets it.

Without a doubt, we can work hard to limit the negative influences in their lives, at least the ones we allow into our home. We can replace negative influences, like music with lyrics that don't affirm our children, with music that offers a positive message. The same applies to entertainment choices.

Let's remember our own influence. **We can be a voice of affirmation and truth by the words we speak to our children.** We can build them up every day. We can model dependence on God for our identity. We can speak words of truth over them and into their situations—consistently and with love.

How can Bible stories and simple devotions shape faith?

Scripture is formative: we learn God's Word, let it dwell in us, and live it out in our everyday rhythms. To help it sink in, we can memorize passages as a family. When we commit God's promises to memory, they take root in our hearts. Scripture renews our minds—equipping children with truth, guiding us with wisdom, and filling us with comfort and hope.

Bible narratives are a joyful entry point for engaging children and teaching biblical truth; thoughtful questions and discussion easily flow from them.

Consider the parable of the prodigal son. Even from a young age, children can understand the basics of the story—that the younger son got into trouble when he disobeyed his father. The older son stayed out of trouble because he obeyed. The story also offers a valuable lesson in forgiveness. Obedience matters, but even when we make poor choices, a good father forgives his children, just as God does.

Discussing the characters of the Bible teaches children how God views them and how much God loves them. The models we present shape young minds and souls. Children learn that they can accomplish remarkable things with God's help and that their lives and choices make a difference personally and in the world around them. These stories teach them to respond to challenges and cultural pressures, and to see their own lives within the larger story of God's work through the ages.

Reading the Bible regularly to children forms an early love and appreciation for God's Word. There are many children's Bible storybooks and children's Bibles. When children are able to read, we can give them faith-based books and Bible activity workbooks. Today, there are many excellent children's publishers offering books for every reading level that teach biblical truth in engaging formats, including comics and graphic novels. Excellent faith-based resources are also available for preteens and teens.

May I encourage you: I purchased lovely books about faith and finding one's identity in God that sat on Willow's shelf for months. Then, one day, she picked one up and read the whole thing—and has read it many times since. I've learned to provide good resources to build her faith and to trust God to draw her to them at the right time.

Lastly, I grew up with family devotions after dinner. We took turns reading a short section each night. That practice shaped me, and I recommend it. Although we haven't adopted that exact habit yet, Willow and I read the Bible or a short devotional at night.

How does church shape family?

We try to attend church every Sunday as a family.

Good churches offer a powerful way to make like-minded friends, connect with local families, and affirm our faith and values. Indeed, families rooted in the church often find their community centered on church friends and events. For us, the church is a source of friendships with those who share our values and moral standards. Having at least a few such friends is vital for children.

If we want our children to value church, we must value it too. There are definitely mornings when I feel like skipping church, but that's a slippery slope. Truthfully, I feel like sleeping in most Sunday mornings! For families who rarely attend church, adding another commitment to the week can feel impossible. But attending church can become part of a weekly routine quite quickly, especially when it's enjoyable and a place to be with friends.

In addition to regular Sunday attendance, we try to keep Willow involved in a weekly Bible-based activity. Many churches offer midweek children's programs and day camps that help children connect, be encouraged, and learn about God.

What do we do when our kids don't want to go to church? If they are young, we need to ask why. Is something or someone making them feel uncomfortable? Sunday school should be a fun place to build friendships and learn about God, so if a young child is not happy, I'd ask plenty of questions and consider switching. In fact, our family changed churches when our daughter was young because the Sunday school wasn't a good fit for her.

Older children go through phases—and, without a doubt, many will reach a stage when they don't want to attend church. When this happens, we need to find out if there is a problem with the church or youth group. What do they think of the teachers and activities? Do they have any friends? Does anything make them feel uncomfortable? Maybe they want to explore a different church, or at least another youth group.

If the youth program is healthy, we can start by expressing why we value church and ask them to stay committed—even if that means attending every other week. Friendships are vital, so what can we do to foster healthy connections with peers in the church?

You can get involved by making positive changes at your church. Could you discuss your child's program with the pastor or priest and offer to help organize more engaging events for the children and youth? Can you invite your child's friends' families to join your church? Perhaps you can organize something at the church or at your home that taps into your child's interests, such as a youth band, a baseball team, a movie night, an air hockey night, or a hike. If you help your youth build strong friendships at church, church will likely become a better experience—and "church" will extend beyond Sunday mornings.

When church is a place of friendship and belonging, our children are more likely to want to be there.

How can we handle entertainment as a family of faith?

At our home, we play Christian music almost exclusively, with occasional classical music. I often find that the theme, message, or language in secular songs is contrary to our values, so I avoid them. In contrast, the lyrics of most Christian songs draw us to think about God, pray, and be grateful. It's uplifting. Our household is noticeably more peaceful, and we are kinder when positive lyrics fill our minds.

When Willow is allowed to watch a show, we choose programming that honors our faith. Is it sometimes boring? Yes. Are there limited options? Yes. Do I tire of slow shows? Yes! Even if I miss watching action movies, I am responsible for what we let into Willow's heart and mind. I don't want to fill her mind with content that undercuts our convictions or normalizes behavior that contradicts our values.

Our simple framework helps: "We choose shows that align with our values."

Thankfully, there are great Christian apps that offer ad-free shows and games for children that align with our faith and family values and teach biblical truth for daily life. When Willow has downtime, I can let her use one of these apps with confidence.

The more I focus our family time on activities that reflect our faith, the more I naturally gravitate away from worldly activities, and the more I feel connected to my family—and grounded in joy and peace.

So yes, it can be annoying to watch slow-paced family movies, but at the same time, I sleep much better afterward, and my mind rests at greater peace.

How do we teach children to navigate culture without compromising values?

We can't shield our children from every secular influence. Children encounter secular music and advertisements that oppose our values—everywhere. At restaurants, at malls. Even in children's spaces, popular music with inappropriate themes plays in the background. We can't control every input, but we can control our response.

The recreation center where Willow takes lessons plays songs that bother her and are not age-appropriate. How can we respond? When we encounter or hear something that Willow recognizes as contrary to our values, we discuss our options: ask to change it, ignore it, or remove ourselves from the situation. When inappropriate songs are played at her recreation program, can she ask the teacher to change the song? If the teacher asks why, is she prepared to articulate a reason that she feels comfortable sharing? Can she endure the situation and try to ignore the lyrics? Or would she rather leave? We have been in all of these situations—asking the teacher to change the song, putting up with a song when the teacher wouldn't change it, and leaving the lesson early.

These situations are never fun to deal with, but they are opportunities for growth. It empowers our children when they learn that there are options for responding—and they know that we fully support them. And what a confidence boost when a child works up the courage to create positive change.

We address other situations by asking questions. For example, when we see bullying, I ask what Willow thinks of how those kids are acting. Since friendship is a huge value to us, I ask, "Do you think the bully has friends?" This question connects to her innate sense of empathy.

Asking "What would you have done in this situation?" helps a child process what they witnessed and prepare for a similar situation in the future. Questions help kids name the value at stake before choosing a response.

There's a commercial we keep encountering right now, featuring gorgeous women who are attracted to men solely because of their scent. Unfortunately, this commercial appears during family-friendly movies. Every time it comes up, I ask Willow if we choose friends based on how they smell. We have a good laugh because it's a ridiculous question. Willow sarcastically answers, "Oh yes, Mom. I *always* choose friends based on how they smell!" So we've been able to evaluate the commercial, recognize the ridiculousness of the emptiness of its message, and diminish its influence by laughing at the absurdity. Humor disarms the message and reinforces our standard.

There are other aspects of culture that we shut out entirely. If specific themes show up in movies or shows, we shut them off. Certain toys and items are not permitted in our home. Anything that gives me a negative feeling, or that looks ugly or creepy, is not welcome in our home. Things related to magic, evil spirits, or any power not from God are thrown away. Being intentional about what we allow into our home and into our child's heart is part of our family framework.

These tools can be applied at all ages. We all find ourselves in situations that run counter to our values. As adults, we can also consider what response is most appropriate for us and take the time to critically analyze the influences around us, including advertisements and media.

We can't control every input—but we can teach a simple response: analyze the influence, consider how it relates to our values, then choose a change when we can, ignore the influence, or leave the situation.

How do we carry everyday faith beyond our front door?

We want to make faith part of our lives every day in every way—including outside our home. What does that look like? For me, this is an area where I'm growing. As soon as I think we've arrived at a new level of faith as a family, I realize we have further to go.

I wonder how I can make my financial habits more faith-based, for instance. One way I incorporate faith into shopping habits is to actively avoid supporting companies that don't share my values. I investigate whether the companies I support align with my values and the lifestyle choices I want my daughter to model in the future. I ask, "Should I bring this product into my home and allow it a place of influence in my family?" It often feels impossible to avoid every company that undermines faith and family.

When we need something, we can ask the Lord to provide it for us according to God's will. I'll note that this habit has been beneficial when Willow wants a new toy or electronic device: we pray for the Lord to provide it, and we accept that the Lord may not. It has been so much easier than having to say no to her many requests. Sometimes the Lord does provide.

Once, I said no to buying another container of bubbles because she kept spilling them, and I felt it was a waste of money. I casually remarked that she could pray for more bubbles. It was Friday. At church that Sunday, a stranger gave her the exact pink bubble bottle that she had asked for! It was an uncanny reminder of how God cares about our efforts to live with integrity—in this case, with our shopping habits—and also cares about Willow's earthly desires, being endlessly patient and gracious toward her.

We have learned to wait on God. We pray for God to provide what we need, then wait and see how God will work.

During the lockdowns, when there was not much to do, my daughter and I began browsing thrift stores. We began to find exactly what we needed. One thing after another on our shopping list appeared— often brand-new and at the perfect time.

One morning, when Willow was four, we came across a cute wooden chair that she immediately liked. We thought about it, and Willow replied that she would prefer a rocking chair. I told her, "We can pray and ask God to provide a rocking chair for you instead, but it might take months. And that's a long, long time."

She said, "That's fine," and that she would ask Jesus for a rocking chair.

Now that probably sounds fine, but we did not stop on the spot to pray. We headed to a second local thrift store.

Would you believe that when we opened the door, right in front of us—a tripping hazard—sat a beautiful, old-fashioned wooden rocking chair, perfectly her size! She was stunned. I was stunned. God answered our prayer. Willow exclaimed (in a voice so loud the whole store heard), "Mom, we didn't even pray out loud yet, but God heard our hearts and answered the prayer of our hearts!"

Praying and then trusting God to provide the items we wanted and needed was my way of modeling trust in God with our finances. This is a principle for life. Finances are just one area we can entrust to God—we can teach our children to bring their needs to God in every area of life.

Another way we show our faith in public is by connecting with the people we see at the grocery store and restaurants. We build relationships with them over time—we remember their names and the details of their lives that they share. Then we can pray for them, encourage them, follow up on what they've shared, and show God's love. Over time, many people in the service industry have said we are their "favorite" customer—and I'm sure it's because they sense that we genuinely care about them and try to bring them joy when we interact with them.

It takes time to develop the habit of incorporating faith into public life. Progress may seem small, but I've learned that God is present in the small things—in the lives we impact, and the ways our family grows through these everyday rhythms.

How far can we go in living counterculturally?

Some say it's impossible to fully live your values. Indeed, although we may want to live by a set of values, we live in a world that sometimes requires us to compromise. We can at least try our best and be aware of how our decisions impact our family.

When we commit to living by our values, we begin to act differently, and our minds open to new possibilities.

I'll share a story about the time we trusted God for something much bigger than a rocking chair. My daughter needed a new bedroom set, but honestly, two to three thousand dollars was ridiculous for a cheap bed frame and side table. I said to my husband, "I don't want to spend more than five hundred. I want beautiful wood, not cheap imported furniture, and I am willing to wait and see what God provides." By this time, we had experienced God providing for our family in many ways, and I felt we should give God the time to work in our lives.

The next morning, Willow and I went thrifting. No bedroom sets. I asked the store manager if there were bedroom sets in the back. He said yes—one would be out on the sales floor the next day.

I didn't know what to expect, but the next day we checked it out. It looked fine, and my husband liked it. The price of the *six-piece* furniture set was three hundred dollars. After it was delivered, I examined it more closely. It was brand-new on the inside—and the maker was a top brand well beyond our means, and, if you can believe it, it was real wood and locally made. Furthermore, the set had little bows engraved along its edges. Perfect for a little girl.

I suppose I shouldn't have been surprised, but it was such a stark example of how God provides for our every need and honors our desires to do what we believe is right. While it is true that I can't always live by my values—sometimes I purchase products from companies I would rather not support—I am amazed at how often God makes it possible for my family to live counterculturally.

I share this story to inspire you to believe more is possible when we bring our needs before God. We begin to see God break through in ways we couldn't have imagined.

The easier path was to buy a cheap bed frame at the original furniture store. It was really hard to walk out of that store. Part of me felt foolish for trying to be overly principled, and I was fearful that I would end up back at the store after a month of trying to avoid paying the full price. I felt angry that life in this world seems to bring one "values" battle after another.

I walked away from this experience realizing afresh that God cares about the seemingly small things in my life, too. **It may be that God wants us to take the risk of waiting and trusting so that we can witness God's great faithfulness.** God is on our side! God knows the struggles of parenting and the challenge of being principled. I believe God desires to partner with us and—when we choose to trust God— we may still face many challenges, but we will also experience many transformative victories.

The challenge? Take one need this month, wait and pray, and see how God provides.

Reflection

1. Where does faith already live in your day? Name one simple daily practice you could add to your family rhythms to build faith and invite God's presence into your home (reciting a blessing, reading a Psalm, praying with your children, texting encouragement from Scripture to family, playing faith-based music or radio).

2. Make prayer a priority by anchoring it in your daily routine. Choose three natural times for short prayers (wake-up, commute, meals, bedtime).

3. What one change would help you be more present with your child (devices away during dinner, notifications off from five to seven p.m., a daily ten-minute play/listen block)? What will you surrender to prioritize presence with your family?

Family Conversation Starters

- "What family needs can we commit to prayer today?"
- "What is the best time during our day to pray together?"
- "What helps each of us sense God's presence?"
- "How can we put our faith into action—show God's love—to friends and family, at school, and at work this week?"

Rhythms for This Week

1. Envision your ideal personal and family prayer rhythm; list three or four goals to grow toward over the next few months.

2. Commit to praying at least once a day; ask God to help you lead your family well and bless them.

3. Swap one daily habit that drains peace with something that brings joy.

4. Find one way to strengthen your child's faith this week.

Four

SIMPLE RHYTHMS FOR A FAMILY THAT FLOURISHES

FAMILY IS THE heartbeat of our lives—our true center.

How special it is when our closest loved ones get our best.

Family is the sacred space where we fully and wholeheartedly live out our faith and turn our desire for a home filled with love, joy, and peace into daily rhythms that shape the ones we love most—so our relationships can truly flourish.

As our faith takes shape in ordinary choices—how we speak, how we show up. We learn to put one another first, to be present, and to love.

As we cultivate kindness, patience, and respect, we learn the depth of God's love for us, and in turn, we extend God's love to those nearest us.

Let's talk about practicing our everyday faith in the daily rhythms and relationships of family life—the place where our values are formed—where they count most and where families truly flourish.

What does it mean to put family first each day?

Prioritizing family comes down to this: choose one another every day. When we choose one another in the ordinary, family wins.

We all have to learn how to put our family before ourselves. This challenge begins with me. It's not easy to think of others first. There are days I want a break from putting my husband and daughter first.

Choosing family first is a daily practice. It means we continually consider the impact of our actions on our family members. The cost of living sacrificially is felt again and again.

I admit—I don't get to do everything I want; I'm constantly interrupted; I do things that bore me for the sake of the family. I have unfulfilled personal goals that I have to surrender to God's timing.

Gradually, we discover that the rewards are greater than the sacrifices we make. Yes, the sacrifices remain unending. But by choosing to spend time with our family, we create memories and find real meaning in life—the soil where love can thrive.

Most of my best times come from activities that slow our family down and let my husband and me live fully in the moment with our daughter. Surprisingly, these moments are some of her best memories, too.

How do we honor our partner while parenting?

A key aspect of putting family first is respecting my husband as our child grows. Respecting him was seamless when Willow was born. But since she started talking, she often interrupts. It's challenging to balance respecting my spouse with responding to my child's every need. This doesn't get easier with time—now I sometimes find myself interrupting my husband to tell my daughter to stop interrupting!

Family first in marriage means honoring each other in public and then working to align our values later in private. We back each other's decisions in the moment, debrief in private, and avoid correcting one another in front of others.

We don't always agree on parenting decisions. These are hard moments. If I'm not happy with what Willow is doing and my husband doesn't correct her, I have to reflect on how to articulate my objections so I can respond with grace and patience. I also have to consider my husband's perspective.

Ultimately, I pick my battles. If it's a moral issue, I will not compromise. If it's not a moral concern, I try to be reasonable and accommodating.

My husband often asked Willow to clean up her things at the very minute we were supposed to leave the house. I value being early and never want to be late, so I found this frustrating; it felt like the wrong time to build a good habit.

I hope I bit my lip and stayed silent—at least I tried. To correct him would have undermined his efforts and initiative as a responsible parent. I humbly admit it turned out well. Because Larry consistently required Willow's room to be clean before we left, Willow learned to race around and tidy her bedroom when we were close to leaving; she knew we wouldn't leave until her room was clean. Now she keeps her room clean without being asked. One day, I talked to her about it. She rolled her eyes and said, "You know how Dad is—can't leave the house until my room is clean." He was right!

I have a gracious and patient husband. We don't often disagree, partly because he has chosen to trust me. Raised in a family of thirteen kids, he tells me, "There are many approaches to raising a child, and if your way won't cause damage, I choose to trust you." That's intimidating because I feel the weight of the responsibility he places on me, but it's empowering to know my husband trusts me. It inspires me to keep giving my best.

For my part, I try to speak kindly of Larry and build him up in front of our daughter. I avoid criticizing him when she is within earshot— or really, ever—and require her to treat him with the same respect I expect toward me.

When a couple chooses to respect each other, children learn how to respect both parents—and the marriage can flourish.

How do we model the value of family for our child?

Modeling the importance of family to children means treating our children as equal members of the family by showing them equal respect. Figuring out what respect means to a child can be a challenge. For a young child, it often means giving our full attention and a listening ear. As they mature, the way to communicate respect goes through changes.

Respecting a child means accepting them as they are, as God made them, and acknowledging their developmental stage. I can respect my daughter by accepting that her voice is naturally loud—and asking her to be quieter only when the setting requires it. When she's excited, I let her finish—even if she's loud—and then coach her on volume. I don't tell her to be quiet all the time.

I show her respect by staying informed about her developmental stage and talking with other moms about their experiences. When Willow was young, I overloaded her with too many questions at once. I asked her to do too many things. She became flustered and frustrated because she was too young to do more than one task at a time. In these moments, respect means being quick to apologize, listen, and seek understanding. At the same time, I remind her to speak to me respectfully and not to raise her voice or be easily angered; this also teaches respect.

When we slow down, stay patient, and listen well, our children feel respected.

Practicing our family values means giving undivided attention when our children talk, putting the phone away during our time together, and being quick to apologize and ask forgiveness when we miss the mark.

We can reinforce the value of family by setting and protecting daily time together. As children grow, there are many things they would rather do than hang out with their parents. It isn't easy to insist on spending time together every day, but it is essential. The struggle is real—games and entertainment can win over sitting at the table or taking a walk together.

Consistency is key. When we forgo family time, it's harder the next day to insist on it.

I accept that prioritizing family time is an ongoing challenge, but as a mother, part of my responsibility is to call our family to it and encourage my child to participate.

We all have other things to do, but when the children move out and begin their own adventures, we will be thankful for every time we invested in being together and every memory we created—the kind that help a family flourish for the long term.

How do we carve out family time when everyone's busy?

I grew up with Family Fun Friday Nights, and I try to carry on that tradition. Whether it's Friday nights or Sunday afternoons, the key is to make family time consistent so that everyone can build their schedules around it. It may take time—even months—to get everyone on the same page, but eventually a family can establish a schedule for sacred time together.

To make Friday nights enjoyable for all of us, I invite Willow and her dad to pick the restaurant, activity, or movie we'll watch. Including them in the plan builds buy-in and gives us all something to look forward to.

We also have daily time together in the morning over coffee, at dinnertime, and after dinner for an hour or two, watching the news or a favorite show. Sometimes we need to handle odds and ends during the evening—like a load of laundry—but our priority is to be present with each other and minimize electronic distractions so connection can deepen.

When should parents put themselves first?

There was a season when I worked so hard to put my family first and to grow in sacrificial love that I neglected myself—and it caught up with me.

I'm embarrassed to admit I often rushed—or skipped—flossing and ended up with a cavity. Similarly, I'd forget simple healthy habits like taking my daily vitamin. So yes, healthy habits are a must, even if my daughter gets frustrated for a moment and has to wait for me. That also means making time for real rest and regular exercise.

A more complex challenge is pursuing my personal goals. Since becoming a mother, I've given minimal attention to some of them. I have little time to study and write, and almost no time to learn Spanish—my lifelong dream. I love spending time with Willow and gladly choose time with her over my own activities. But is there a way to do both? One solution is to schedule shared reading time: she can read her books while I study or write. It's a small window, but it's a start.

As she grows, I look forward to sharing goals—this will take planning and a bit of convincing, but it can happen.

Parents have basic needs that must be met alongside our children's needs, so we stay healthy and able to parent well. Caring for ourselves is one way we care for our families—and it helps our homes flourish.

How can we approach frustrating everyday tasks with love?

My most frustrating everyday task is running errands together. I often want to run out to the grocery store by myself. A bit of alone time. A few minutes of quiet "me time," a five-minute drive to think or pray.

But my daughter *always* wants to go with me. Every parent knows how much more effort it takes to include a child. And there's no quiet time—no peace of mind.

I try not to dwell on the inconvenience; while it's tiring to go without alone time, I'm grateful my child isn't watching TV—and even more grateful that she wants to be with me.

When Willow was little, she said to me, "Mom, you are the best mom in the world because you always take me with you and never leave me behind." It melted my heart. For all those times I was irritated and begrudgingly packed her into the car—she was thinking, *What a great mom I have!*

It was a humbling reminder to appreciate every moment.

The tasks we dislike often become the very moments that give life meaning.

Finally, seasons change. Willow is older now and often reads in the car. I miss her little voice chatting away. At the grocery store, she is so helpful at getting the items on our list, but I miss when she wanted to be carried. Sometimes she prefers to stay home with Larry, and I do get alone time—but it's less enjoyable than I expected.

Is support from extended family essential?

Ideally, extended family—especially those we see often—support us as we establish family values with our children. It's difficult to implement household rules without that support—so explaining the "why" and potential benefits behind our rules matters. A short, gracious heads-up about the new rhythms we're forming before family gatherings also helps.

For example: "We're keeping devices away at dinner so we can be fully present and talk." If our parents bring devices, tension can follow. I give extended family space and comment only when it affects my daughter. If Willow is invited to look at a phone, I address her kindly, not the adult: "Willow, I'd like you to wait until after dinner to look at Papa's phone, and while we are together, let's chat." Speaking to the child in the moment is respectful, keeps the focus on the situation, and avoids preaching or embarrassing relatives. Later, I might quietly follow up with my relatives: "We're building a no-devices-at-dinner habit with Willow. I'd appreciate your help. Could we all keep our phones away from the table while she's present?"

When relatives make an effort to support our family values, we can thank them. When possible, invite feedback and suggestions. This signals that we value their perspective and recognize their influence, and it opens the door to nonconfrontational conversations about our values. When extended family understands our values, they are more likely to support us. **Even imperfect support strengthens what we're building at home.**

Over time, our values become clear, and others can choose how to respond. I can't control their responses, but I remain responsible for guiding my family with kindness and consistency.

We do what we can to bring grandparents on board. In strained family relationships, we pray, practice patience, and remember that much can change with time. We wait for the right moment to address our concerns and limit requests to how they are around our children. This might mean ignoring their device use at a couples' dinner but gently speaking up when our children are present.

When conflict arises, we can trust God to soften hearts and bring about good for all involved, even in the most complicated situations and relationships so that peace can flourish in our family.

How can grandparents support our mission to raise kids by our values?

The world has changed significantly since our parents were raising us. Grandparents' parenting experiences differ from those of parents today. They didn't have to address online learning, the invasion of personal electronic devices, the pressures of social media, or school curricula that clashed with their values. Even familiar issues, like bullying and mental health concerns, took different forms.

All of this means that, generally speaking, grandparents didn't experience the same challenges that are now front and center. So it's understandable when our perspectives don't align and generational gaps surface.

Parents may wonder if grandparents can offer valuable solutions to today's problems. Yet we can find common ground—our life circumstances may seem very different, but the core of many of our experiences and challenges is similar. Like our parents, we haven't lived through the same pressures our children face, so we share that feeling of being disconnected from the younger generation. Leaning into that shared humility can become a bridge.

We're all learning as we go. A simple starting point for partnering is to admit that we're a little uncertain how best to raise this generation—and to choose grace over judgment while we figure things out together. **Name the shared goal—"We both want what's best for the kids"—then work out the details.**

Here's what partnering looked like for me. There are moments when my dad really enjoys watching videos with Willow on his phone. That frustrates me, because I want us to spend time talking and being together—not directing our attention toward a phone. However, watching videos and discussing them afterward creates valuable shared memories for my dad. When he told me this, I saw his heart—and my perspective shifted.

How can I show my dad understanding and respect while upholding my values and preferences in this situation? Our compromise is that Willow doesn't hold the phone, and video-watching is limited to about half an hour. This example may seem obvious; it wasn't for me. I struggled to uphold my values while respecting what was meaningful to my dad.

Close family relationships are complex. I try to keep in mind that I want my parents in my life, I need their support, and I want to foster a beautiful and positive relationship between my daughter and her grandparents. I hope my parents will be in my life for many more years, so this is a relationship well worth the hard work to preserve.

I'll end with a short story. We moved into a condo and discovered that it was essentially a retirement home. My daughter was the youngest in the building at six weeks old, and I was the second youngest. Many residents were in their eighties and nineties. They loved to stop and chat when they saw the baby and always offered the same one-line life advice: "Appreciate every moment. Life goes by so fast."

Those little daily reminders were a helpful guide and deepened my appreciation for the wisdom and perspective of those who've walked the road before us.

What can we do to build a good relationship with our children's grandparents?

As parents, we can recognize the value grandparents offer. Grandparents matter deeply to children.

Model the respect toward our parents that we want our children to show toward us when we're older. Our children, who are always watching, will likely follow our example.

When it is "safe" and wise, we can ask our parents for help. We can be honest about what we need, share our perspective, and ask for feedback and guidance.

We can thank them when we notice their efforts to invest in the family.

Like all of us, grandparents have struggles. **We may need to reach a place where we have no expectations, simply choosing to be grateful for the good moments without expecting change.**

I'm learning that sometimes having fewer expectations helps me find joy in the good moments while removing the heartache of disappointment. When we hold fewer expectations, we can experience less pain and fewer sleepless nights.

This posture has brought freedom to many of my friends. It transforms us—we discover greater peace, and ironically, our relationships with our parents often grow stronger and begin to flourish.

What can grandparents do to build a good relationship with us as parents?

Grandparents, your impact and influence are immense—often greater than you realize.

I find that new parents feel a great need for help from grandparents. The comment I hear most is that a new baby brings big challenges—feeding, basic care, exhaustion, medical decisions. Unexpected confusion and hurt can follow when well-meaning mothers or relatives give them "space" they didn't request. Many friends say their moms came to see the baby and stayed for dinner, but didn't offer help, creating more work for an already overwhelmed mom.

It can be hard to know exactly what to do. Grandparents can ask, **"What would be most helpful right now?"** Offer practical help: wash the dishes, bring groceries, mow the lawn, get the car washed, fold laundry. Help in the ways parents prefer. **Serving builds trust and gratitude.**

Sometimes your adult child needs your companionship and compassion most. Sit with them, listen more than you speak, and resist the urge to "fix" everything in one visit.

Offer encouragement. No parent gets everything right, so look for ways to affirm that you see us doing our best. When parents feel affirmed, they may be more likely to welcome your advice. It may take time.

In my experience, moms need their moms—and dads need their parents as well. We need support; we need affirmation. Grandparents, if your relationship with your son or daughter is strained, now is the time to reach out, even if only for your grandchildren's sake.

Parenting is hard today; your wisdom, love, and support are deeply needed. Your impact, whether positive or negative, is enormous.

Your steady presence can make the load of parenting feel lighter and the home more peaceful so families can flourish.

How meaningful are friendships?

For years, my extended family lived in another country, so friendships were our lifeline. Out of necessity, my friends became like sisters. We work hard to build strong bonds. We take the time to talk on the phone and meet in person whenever possible.

When I faced severe anxiety and depression after a car crash, community was essential to my recovery. The steady support of family and friends carried me. Later, during lockdowns, isolation re-triggered my anxiety and depression. Once again, friendship and community sustained me.

There is healing in friendships—in being held and hugged. If we feel isolated and don't have close friends to comfort us, we can take one small step to connect. Invite someone for coffee. Meet at the park with the kids. Call after the kids are in bed. Go for a walk with a neighbor. Plan a game night with another family.

We weren't made to live without connection. Relationships give our lives meaning, remind us we're not alone, and hold us together when life comes apart.

We parent best when we're supported by people who share our values. We all need someone who knows us, cheers us on, and sees how hard we're trying.

How do friends support faith-based, family-centered parenting?

Like-minded friends are essential to our family life. I work hard to nurture those connections.

I am grateful for a handful of friends who join us in pushing back against unhelpful cultural pressures on our children. We seek friendships that share our faith and place our kids in settings where their faith is affirmed and they are accepted for who they are.

I remember Willow's first time memorizing a Bible verse. We added hand motions that she loved practicing. When her friend visited, Willow began, "I can do"—and her friend squealed and joined her in reciting the whole verse. They were delighted. I know Willow differs in many ways from those around her, and our family rules differ from most of her friends'. Seeing these two little ones share a sacred moment was a gift.

We may not have many friends who share our values, but the few who do are deeply cherished and help our children's faith to flourish.

Reflection

1. How do you show respect to each family member (words, tone, time, and privacy)? Name one way you'll show greater respect this week so your relationships can flourish.

_____

_____

_____

_____

_____

2. What simple routine could you add to deepen family connection (e.g., a Friday game night, a Sunday walk, device-free dinners)? Make a simple plan to start.

_____

_____

_____

_____

_____

3. When a choice or comment from friends or family undermines your values and family rules, how will you respond graciously and clearly in the moment?

4. Who are your like-minded, values-aligned friends? Take one concrete step this week to nurture a meaningful bond.

Family Conversation Starters

- "What makes you feel respected? What makes you feel disrespected?"
- "What activity could we do together this week that would bring us joy?"
- "What are practical ways we can put each other first this week?"
- "When someone pressures us to act against our values, how should we respond?"

Rhythms for This Week

1. Find a private moment with each member of your family to affirm them in one concrete way. Thank close extended family members for one way they bless your family. Check your heart for bitterness or resentment; surrender it to God, and ask for forgiveness and love to take its place so peace can flourish.

2. Put one family activity on next week's calendar, and choose a regular time to reserve for quality time together. Note it here.

3. What is one step you can take to nurture a values-aligned friendship? Pray for a companion to share your journey of leading well.

Five

SIMPLE RHYTHMS FOR A HOME THAT THRIVES

NURTURING OUR HEALTH and wholeness is our family's third core value and helps our home thrive. It shapes every aspect of our lives—spiritual, emotional, mental, and physical. Staying healthy places us in a better posture to serve others more freely and thrive together.

I believe God has a unique plan and purpose for every family. We all have limitations, and by God's grace we're growing—emotionally and spiritually. We're on a lifelong journey to become all God desires us to be.

We don't aim for perfection; we aim for faithfulness—making healthy choices as often as we can with the knowledge we have now.

Being whole means attending to the person God made each of us to be. We develop our strengths, address our limitations, and find peace in our God-given identity in Christ.

It's easy to compare ourselves and long for what others have. Instead, we lean into gratitude for who God made us to be and for the family God has given us.

As we tend to our health and well-being, we position ourselves to serve and support others. From a faith-based perspective, we seek to serve our family, friends, and community by sharing God's love in word and action. This value shows up in the daily choices we make, and when faith anchors our health, our family learns to choose what is life-giving and thrives.

Together, we pursue wholeness not to perfect ourselves but to be ready for the good works God has prepared for us.

Where does the journey toward healthier living begin?

Incorporating a healthy lifestyle into our daily rhythms is an ongoing challenge. There are factors we can't fully know and control—the quality of our air, food, and water, and the constant wireless signals from our devices. In our home, healthy living is an act of stewardship, not a goal of perfection. It's a response to God's goodness, not a quest for control. We pay attention to the choices we make and ask for God's guidance. We aim to serve God and one another faithfully, and wise, healthy decisions help us give our best and thrive.

Helping our families stay healthy starts with being well-informed. What's in our food, and what are the potential risks associated with food dyes, colors, and ingredients we can't even pronounce? What are the chemicals in products we use every day, from cleaning supplies and personal care items to plastics and children's toys?

It can feel overwhelming. So we start small: pick one area at a time, learn a little, and make one better choice.

Recently, I was feeling jittery every night. Something was wrong. Sure enough, I reread the label of a new snack I had started eating, and noticed an ingredient I react to. I stopped eating the snack, and my jitters didn't return. It's hard to find healthy snacks and to check every label. But feeling anxious was worse.

My journey toward greater health began with paying attention—becoming informed and more aware of my environment, diet, and daily habits. Once informed, I could make better choices for our family that align with our value of health and wholeness. We don't have to learn everything at once; each week we can learn a little more, make the next choice a bit wiser than the last, and thank God for the progress as our home thrives.

What "rules to live by" can guide a family's health?

We've established simple, repeatable "rules to live by" for what we eat, the activities we choose, and the environments we spend time in—guidelines that keep us aligned with our values and make daily decisions simpler.

We prioritize whole, minimally processed foods—plenty of fruits and vegetables—and avoid ingredients that don't serve our health. We schedule healthy activities each week. To the best of our ability, we spend time in places that reflect God's creation, and we limit our time in areas that are device-dense, heavily polluted, or otherwise unhealthy.

These rules are our way of stewarding the bodies God gave us. Our goal is to choose our diet and activities wisely, stay mindful of our environment, and give ourselves grace when we fall short.

How can we keep eating healthy at home simple?

When Willow was young, I gave her a simple family rule: we eat foods God made.

This means choosing foods from nature, especially fruits, vegetables, meats, and dairy—and enjoying them in whole or minimally processed forms whenever possible. We avoid processed foods and artificial dyes, and we scan labels for additives we consider unhealthy.

We find that taking short, frequent trips to the grocery store, rather than one big trip, keeps fresh foods on hand. I want my family and guests to eat well, so I need to keep healthy options within reach at home.

How can we navigate limited food options without missing out?

It can feel limiting at first—especially at events—so we plan for it. Take birthday parties, for example: the food (even with "white" icing) is often full of artificial colors and refined sugar. At such events, we notice how different our diet can be. We usually eat a little beforehand and offer to bring a shareable option, like a fruit platter.

At home, we aren't aware of the limitations because our diet has become a lifestyle. Willow knows our family values, so it is simply our way of being.

It's also freeing. We don't have much appetite for junk food, and we love fruit, sometimes with a little whipped cream. We don't experience sugar highs that leave us feeling out of control, or the behavior struggles that can follow the consumption of artificial colors and excess sugar. We appreciate feeling calm and in control of our emotions.

Limited options encourage us to buy a variety of fruits and vegetables. We invest in tasty, high-quality meats, rather than "treats" that aren't healthy and offer only temporary satisfaction.

Once we committed to this way of eating, it no longer felt limiting; there's so much God has given to us to enjoy and help us thrive.

How can we empower children to eat more healthily?

Helping a child embrace healthy eating is one of the most common struggles I see in families.

Here are a few practices that help in our home.

Groceries. **What we buy and bring into the home is what the family eats.** We can skip buying junk food and make sure to have fruit and other healthy options. I drop by the grocery store every two to three days for a quick pickup of fruit and essentials, with a full shop as needed. Asking Willow which fruit she wants helps her take ownership. If we see some fruit she hasn't tried, we might purchase it for "fun" and food exploration.

Most families love treats and desserts. Our approach is to bake quick, healthy desserts or choose high-quality store-bought ones. A local bakery can be a great place to purchase homemade desserts. One benefit is that richer, better ingredients mean a smaller piece satisfies.

A rule of our home is that Willow must eat her dinner meal— whether at dinner, later that night, or the next morning. In other words, dinner is the next thing she eats. This is important because it's her healthiest, most complete meal, and if she doesn't eat it, she may go straight to sugary snacks. It's also manageable—I've learned to serve reasonable portions. I cook the veggies the way she likes them, which is sautéed in butter and a bit of garlic, or baked with some cheese and light herbs. Only once did she eat a cold dinner for breakfast. After a bite or two, she learned her lesson—the experience motivated her to eat when the meal is fresh.

Another tip is to give the child choices. I ask Willow what vege-tables she wants us to buy at the store. After the usual response of "nothing," she chooses two or three items. I let her pick them out and bag them, if she wants to. As I plan dinner, I ask Willow which partic-ular vegetable she wants that night and how she wants it cooked. Offering two good options, such as broccoli or carrots, helps her feel part of our decision-making. All of this gives her some ownership over her diet and makes it more likely that she'll eat her dinner.

Willow is rewarded for eating her dinner with a tasty dessert almost every night. I know this would not be best for some families. If the kids need to go to bed right away, perhaps a handful of their favorite fruit can serve as a treat, helping them meet their daily nutri-ent intake.

This leads me to a friend's tip. Her boys "hate" vegetables, so she serves fruit instead. Now, I often serve fruit or another item that isn't traditionally a dinner side, like cucumbers—options Willow likes.

Taste buds take time to develop a liking to a new food. We shouldn't be surprised if we don't initially enjoy a food item. We can encourage our kids to keep trying it until their bodies develop a liking for it. I've found Willow often needs to try a new vegetable three or four times before she starts to like it; even if she hesitates to admit it, I can tell she's warming to it.

None of these tips ensure that meals will be easy! It isn't easy to motivate myself to have healthy meals every night, either. I some-times want to take the easier route of foods Willow would prefer and avoid the endless conversations about the benefits of healthy eating. But the work of providing healthy food and promoting a healthy diet is an investment in our present and future well-being.

In the end, small, steady choices—clear rules, real food, and kid-sized ownership—teach our children how to nourish the bodies God gave them so they can thrive.

How do activities reflect a commitment to health?

We know that getting outdoors and being active help us thrive. Like other healthy habits, we can incorporate outdoor time and exercise into our daily lives in small, consistent ways—by building them into our routines.

My husband's physical injuries from our car accident limit our options, so we make sure Willow is enrolled in two or three local programs or teams each week. That's especially important as a homeschooled child.

A friend shared that she tells her three kids, "Okay, time to go play outside!" every day. Almost without exception, they spend an hour outside. It gives her needed quiet, too. She says this habit is so ingrained in the family routine that the kids rarely complain.

Our version is a short park stop after dinner: Willow can run around, and my husband and I can sit and talk. Even fifteen to twenty minutes together is beneficial.

When it comes to spending time outside, sadly, it can be hard to avoid air and water pollution. We try to be aware of other factors, too. We avoid a local sports center because it's located beside a high-voltage substation, and the fields are sprayed heavily with chemicals. When possible, we choose parks with trees and natural surfaces.

We do our best within reason, and we pray as a family for God's protection every day. It's just a sentence or two, but it gives me peace to trust God when I fail and for protection from unseen dangers. This rhythm keeps our health choices grounded in faith rather than fear.

How can we set healthy, values-based rhythms for electronic devices?

Before setting boundaries for electronics, we reflect on the role we want devices to have in our family and the purpose they should serve. My reflection leads to concerns about the impact of devices on our family. We know many are designed to be addictive, and overuse can affect our emotional well-being. Using a device is often a solo activity that isolates users. Then there is the content—the negative influences children may be exposed to, including those found in advertisements. We also consider exposure to wireless signals (Wi-Fi, cellular, Bluetooth).

All of this feels at odds with what I want for my family. So I shifted my thinking from "How much screen time is permissible?" to "What do we want our family to focus on?"—and it isn't devices. I chose to reflect on my values and how our device usage could align with them.

Our guiding principle is to use devices to serve our lives and support our values of faith, family, and health.

I appreciate the educational possibilities that devices offer. Educational devices can teach kids about the world and help with reading, math, telling time—so much. But we said no to personal electronics until Willow was seven. I didn't want Willow using gadgets with wireless signals or becoming addicted to screens while she was young and especially sensitive. She was allowed—and encouraged—to video-call family members, but she had to leave my iPad on its EMF-blocking stand. The iPad remained a tool to connect us to family rather than a toy.

That was it. It's much easier to have a blanket rule that is rarely broken. It becomes a way of life, reducing the constant "Can I use it, and for how long?" decisions. Fewer on-the-spot decisions mean reduced stress for everyone.

When she turned seven, I was willing for her to engage in several educational tools, but they wouldn't work on our old iPad. We upgraded to a new family iPad. We set safeguards: a password (so she can't use it without my knowing) and limited apps. We require her to ask before switching apps and to use the iPad only in shared spaces whenever possible. I want to be able to hear what she is listening to and see the screen at any time.

In short, we've found it's best to delay electronics as long as possible, and then strictly limit access, time, and content so attention and relationships can thrive.

How can we enforce clear, simple limits on electronics—and keep the peace?

Setting healthy device limits is challenging. When kids beg for the latest gadgets or more time—wanting what "all the other kids" have—it's frustrating.

There comes a time to pause, step back, and reset our approach. A few practices help.

Explain the "why." We can explain why we limit device use. If a child gets upset when we say device time is over, that's a perfect teaching moment. Devices can be addictive; the resistance when Mom and Dad say time's up is precisely why limits matter. If children understand the "why," it helps them follow the rules and models thoughtful decision-making.

Define a simple time window. Perhaps devices are off-limits until chores and homework are complete. Game time happens in one predictable daily slot and is limited to games and apps that Mom and Dad approve. We can switch to ad-free, faith-based apps. If we get complaints, we may shave time off the next day to show that our limits are dependable. To save us from nagging, we can ask our children to set a timer to alert them when time is up.

Provide positive device options. We can source faith-based apps with no advertising. The shows and games are educational and engaging, and they align with faith and family values. This reassures us that device use won't undermine our values; instead, the content reinforces them.

Keep phone privileges narrow. We can limit the ways our children can use our phones—perhaps only the camera and music app are permitted. We can make the situation easier by removing game apps on our phones. Any limits parents set for their phones are better than giving children full access.

Offer substitutes. This is essential. In our family, we provide non-screen tools: Willow has a traditional watch (actually three) and two cameras, in part so that she can't complain that she doesn't have these. Her camera isn't connected to Wi-Fi but does have a few simple games—a much better alternative to my phone. We keep a bag of books and activities in the car and rotate fresh finds from the thrift store and library. It takes effort, but it's worth avoiding the default to screens. When friends visit, we can turn to our stack of board and card games and set up special activities like our pottery wheel.

Let kids be a part of finding alternatives. Even little ones can help find other activities to do and games to play. As children grow older, they can engage in more complex activities that stimulate their minds and spark their creativity. They can learn a new hobby or skill. Eventually, we can guide children to set limits for themselves regarding electronic devices. This helps them develop self-control, self-regulation, and a sense of time.

Make conversation the "default app." We can turn off devices simply to talk and be together. In the car, I tell Willow I'd rather chat with her than let her use a device. It doesn't matter the topic—I just want to talk with her because she matters. I love her voice and want to know her thoughts.

Plan for restaurants. If adults talk and kids feel ignored, boredom often leads to screen time. In my experience, the best way to engage children is to include them in the conversation or play games like tic-tac-toe on the menu. With other adults, inclusion isn't always natural—then an activity bag helps. Electronics can be a last resort—until the meal arrives.

Stay consistent. Children are resilient and love to repeat the same requests. We can hold the line kindly and revisit our reasons for having device-use limits. We need only be a *little* stronger than our children.

Every family is different in what they allow. Whatever rules a family decides on, we can have alternative activities on hand, engage the children so they are not left out of conversation, and set clear limits on when devices are allowed and what they're for, with clear consequences if boundaries are not respected so that peace and presence can thrive.

Should we be concerned about EMF emissions from everyday devices?

We want to understand how the devices we use every day behave—what they emit when connected to Wi-Fi, while charging, and when held close to the body. Start by learning the basics and consulting balanced, science-based sources. Look into the sensitivity of children's brains and bodies to these emissions.

There's no need to overstate the dangers, but we can acknowledge that children are often unaware of these invisible risks, and it's our job to protect them. When I see babies sucking on a phone, it pains me—surely there are better options.

When I committed to treating my phone as a transmitter and limiting Willow's close contact, I made positive changes, like buying a case marketed as an EMF-reducing shield for family calls. When she wants to look at our photos or use the camera, I switch to airplane mode to turn off connectivity. We have a simple phone stand for her to use during video calls so she doesn't have to hold the phone.

I purchased an EMF meter to check the EMF levels in our home. That led me to realize that our smart meter was mounted near Willow's room. A quick fix was to sew a layer of conductive (Faraday) fabric onto the back of her curtain at that spot.

For me, this comes back to stewardship and responsibility before God. It is our duty to protect our children's physical well-being, and we can do our best. If we can make their environment a little safer and calmer, we should—and then we can trust God with what we cannot see or control. If our children's environment is safer, then they will be happier too.

How do friends and family respond to screen rules?

The response to our choice to avoid personal electronics, especially when we're with friends, has been surprisingly positive.

Often, when Willow is with friends, they're on their devices. Willow knows she isn't allowed to use their devices, so she pulls out her activity bag. Within a minute, her friends are more interested in what Willow has in her bag—usually activity books and games—than their devices.

In my experience, **kids are much happier and more engaged in hands-on activities with friends than playing solo on a device.**

Not everyone remembers our family rules. When relatives or friends want to show Willow photos or videos on their phones—or worse, introduce a game to her—it often presents a challenge for me. When we see our extended family, just as with friends, we want our time together to be meaningful. I also need to remember that sharing photos is meaningful for them, so I need to be flexible. We avoid scrolling and passive video-watching, but we'll allow a couple of minutes to view a special photo or brief clip—especially when it connects us to people we love.

Finally, we accept that some people—for whatever reasons—disagree with our approach. That's true of many parenting choices. I try to remember that the friends who understand our "why" and respect our choices are the ones whose relationships endure.

Most often, people simply adapt. When they're around Willow, I often hear other parents tell their kids, "Put your phones away until we leave." That's not a bad thing.

How can our values guide our everyday entertainment choices?

In setting standards for entertainment choices, we can return to our core values and create guidelines we can easily apply—and that our children can understand.

Children mimic what they see, even when they don't fully understand it. At the park, an upbeat song can prompt little ones to imitate suggestive dance moves—they're mirroring what they've watched. When Willow seems engrossed in play, a comment between my husband and me can prompt her to chime in—a reminder that she's always listening.

It's tempting to assume, "They don't understand, so it won't stick," but children absorb patterns, tone, and attitudes long before they can explain them.

We are committed to carefully choosing what we let in and reviewing entertainment options through the filter of our values—faith, family, and health and wholeness. Holding these values in mind best equips me to evaluate a given movie, show, or song. Then, we review the description and trailer.

For example, when a new movie comes out, we can ask: Does it align with our faith? Does it honor family? Does it support whole-person health? If the movie doesn't seem to conflict with our values, we consider it.

We can't be sure that a movie aligns with our values until we watch it. This is one reason why it's important to watch movies together as a family. When a child acts nervously and we see that they are uncomfortable, we turn it off. When we find ourselves watching something that doesn't sit right, we turn it off. Those moments can feel inconvenient, but they let us model self-regulation and discernment.

It isn't straightforward or easy. In our home, we strive to consistently apply our values filter while allowing for our daughter's growth. When we've watched something that we later regret, we discuss it, and I share why I feel the content didn't align with our values. I apologize to Willow for allowing her to view a scene that may have upset her—so she knows I take my parenting role seriously and I can be trusted to guide her in the right direction.

How do entertainment guidelines play out in daily life?

We use a few excellent free apps that offer faith-based, family-friendly movies and shows. I'm grateful there are so many faith-based and family-friendly options.

Beyond that, a few contemporary movies pass our filter of faith, family, and health. As Willow matures, we gradually loosen some standards as she learns to recognize content that doesn't align with our values and chooses not to imitate it. For example, we may overlook occasional mild language because Willow doesn't repeat it.

We also consider our child's temperament. Animal-on-animal action (e.g., dinosaurs) has never bothered her, so we permit some movies other families might skip. Every family discerns what's best for them.

Gratefully, we've discovered many gems from yesteryear. Shows like *Black Beauty* and *Little House on the Prairie* are sweet and teach us about the past. I admit many of these shows feel painfully slow-paced. But the benefit is that none of us is silently glued to the screen. We can talk during the show and do other things, even play a game.

Is Willow missing out? In some ways, yes. She's also missing messages we don't want shaping her heart. Recent box-office misses indicate that many families opt out when a film's message clashes with their values—we know we are not alone in what we keep out.

In the end, we choose what we let in, so our home stays aligned with faith and family. We choose entertainment that affirms our beliefs and helps our child flourish and thrive.

How does your child respond to the value of healthy living?

Our family was blessed with the opportunity to begin teaching healthy rhythms when our daughter was a toddler. Since this is how we live, Willow accepts it as our norm.

A situation opened her eyes to the value of health. A friend gave her candy while I wasn't there. Willow was hesitant to eat it, but my friend assured her it was fine. Willow had never had dyes before, and her body reacted strongly—she became hyperactive, ran around for hours, and remained wide awake past midnight. I tried to get her to settle, but she complained, "Mommy, that candy won't let me stop moving." She was miserable and never forgot the experience.

At restaurants, we observe kids on devices who seem disconnected from the table conversation. Sometimes they don't respond to greetings or servers, or they speak loudly because they are wearing headphones. We talk about whether the screen adds to their joy or pulls them away from the moment. We contrast that situation with families who are connecting with each other, laughing, and savoring their meals. These moments help Willow understand and accept the healthy rhythms we've established.

I know she would like a phone, and she expresses frustration that other kids seem to eat whatever they want. I explain—again—why I want her to be healthy and that every family is different and has its own rules.

Sometimes we have to play the "parent card" and trust that one day our children will be grateful for the choices we have made for our family.

How can we raise a child to stand apart without standing alone?

Ultimately, we want our children to lead—not follow—as they become all God designed them to be.

Each child is unique and always will be. Neither adopting nor resisting cultural norms changes that. **We can teach our children to stand up as leaders and celebrate who God made them to be. That means they'll stand out among their peers and in society.** To keep them from standing alone, we cultivate friendships rooted in shared values.

Empowering children to lead starts with equipping them with the truth—equipping them to articulate their values. Knowing the "why" is key. They need to own the truth to stand by it. For children to *choose* what's right, they need to understand the consequences—dishonesty breaks trust, inappropriate images leave lasting impacts, and unkind comments harm friendships.

Next, we practice so that children learn to articulate their values and stand up for the truth. At home, role-playing can help children practice saying no and debating in a safe environment as they develop their skills and build confidence.

When situations feel hard or intimidating, we ask God for strength and courage to do what's right, and we remind ourselves that God is always with us, protecting us. There is blessing in shining the light of Christ.

The effort to raise Willow this way has borne fruit. It shows up when she draws her friends away from devices and invites them to engage in real-world activities. It's rewarding to witness. My job is easier, and I am happy she is having a positive impact on other families, who associate our time together with being outside, doing new crafts, or playing games.

This is leadership taking root. We're not raising her to fit in; we're raising her to live faithfully and invite others to join her.

When we value our health, we naturally develop healthier habits. Peace follows because our rhythms echo our convictions—and when those values rest on faith, that peace deepens. Our home thrives.

Reflection

1. Are there ways you are neglecting your health? What are the top changes you need to make for healthier living? How could these changes help you and your family thrive?

2. What practical changes would provide healthier eating options for your family so everyone can thrive day by day?

3. What simple "family rules to live by" for screen time and entertainment choices would make your family's daily decisions easier and help your kids thrive?

4. How can you lead well in the areas where you want your family to be healthier and thriving together?

Family Conversation Starters

- "What does healthy eating look like? What are the benefits of healthy eating? How does healthy eating honor God? How can we improve in this area so our bodies and minds thrive?"
- "What boundaries will we practice for screen time?"
- "What activities do we each enjoy that can replace screen time? When we're with friends, what three activities could we enjoy together instead of screens?"
- "What guidelines help us decide what to watch and which electronic games to play?
- "When a song, show, or ad feels wrong, how should we respond? What can we do if something feels wrong at school? With friends?"

Rhythms for This Week

1. With your family, discuss and agree on simple "rules to live by" for food, screen time, and entertainment—then write them down as a shared plan for thriving.

2. What practical steps can you take to have healthy food options at home and ready-to-go for the road?

3. How can you plan for non-screen activities (such as activity bags for young children; books and supplies to support hobbies for older children)?

Six

SIMPLE RHYTHMS FOR CONNECTION AMID HURRY, NOISE, AND BUSYNESS

AFTER I BEGAN weaving the values of faith, family, and health and wholeness into our daily rhythms, I became more aware of the moments my actions didn't align—a gap between my desire to stay connected and the pull of distractions. Hurry, noise, screens, and impatience kept undermining my efforts to build a close, lasting bond with my daughter.

I felt stressed out and overwhelmed; I needed a change amid the busyness.

Could my days consistently reflect my faith? Could my actions match the love and care I feel for my family?

This chapter identifies the everyday struggles parents face when trying to live by their values and offers simple, practical rhythms that bring joy, peace, and deeper connection with one another and God—habits that help us stay connected even when life gets loud.

Here is the honest journey God used to shape me into the mother I long to be: listening when it's inconvenient, practicing presence, cultivating patience, choosing gentleness over anger, navigating tricky friendships with wisdom, and safeguarding our family's privacy.

How can we build a deeper connection with children?

Building deeper connections begins with the basics: **listening and showing genuine interest.** We can listen and listen and listen some more. We can resist the urge to interrupt our children, especially when the moments our children talk are rare—particularly amid hurry and noise. Then we show interest. When our children resist, we need to be intentional and persistent.

One of my best friends often says, **"Tell me everything."** At first, I didn't believe her. But she won me over by constantly showing that she cares deeply about whatever is on my heart, and I know that she truly wants to know all the details. I started using the line on Willow. If I say, "How was your day?" I get the usual "good." But when I say, "Tell me everything!" her face lights up. She is a talker, and now it's her moment to shine. Willow dives into the details with a full play-by-play.

Sometimes it doesn't work—I get an eye roll instead. That's okay. I'll say: "Tell me something!" By showing interest, Willow knows I care. Usually, the details come. Other times, it's a battle to get a response beyond "good." When a child hesitates to share, it may mean something has made them feel uncomfortable—a cue to circle back privately later.

Another best friend is a proponent of detailed questions. She receives the best responses when she asks her children specific questions: "What was upsetting today?" "What brought you joy today?" "What made you laugh?" "What was your best moment?"

I've learned that getting an answer is less important than our taking the time to ask, listen, and show that we care.

Invest time. Spending time together is so important to children. We can keep it simple. What is our child doing right now? We can join them. Little kids are easy—they want to be included and for us to be present and play with them.

For older kids, what interests them? It can be hard to tell. Watch how they spend time, and look for chances to learn about their interests if they won't say. Is your child trying to get in better shape? Join them for a walk or workout. Maybe join a gym as a "thing" that brings you together. Are they exploring a special diet? Go with them to a health food store. Are they obsessing over something like alien films? Watch one with them.

You may not have the opportunity to talk with them while doing the activity, but showing interest signals that you care. If you have no interest in aliens, yet you watch the whole movie without checking your device, they will see that you are invested. And afterward you'll have something to talk about—aliens!

Another idea: **invite them to join you** for some of your activities. You might assume that your child has no interest in the things that interest you. But if you invite them to join you, you show that you want to spend time with them. And they might say yes! If your relationship is strained right now, they may be unlikely to ask you if they can join in what you're doing. Or they may feel rejected because of personal issues they are dealing with. So just invite them. Risk a no.

The risk of trying to connect with your child is worth the chance that it will create an opportunity for a more meaningful relationship. We can keep showing up, keep listening, and keep choosing presence—staying connected amid the busyness—and pray for connection to grow in the small, faithful moments.

How can we help children open up to us?

The most effective way to initiate conversation is to establish rhythms and routines that keep us connected. Encouraging children to open up in the early years is vital; it sets a pattern for life. Little ones naturally love sharing and playful prompts—as simple as "Okay, don't *tell* me—*whisper* it"—can make sharing fun.

We can carve out sacred time together and make the most of it in our daily routines. Driving is a natural time to chat. On drives, I often play a game with Willow called "either/or," which offers a window into Willow's thoughts. I once asked, "Indoor playground or outdoor park?" She chose the outdoor park—then complained about a boy at our indoor park who was "always chasing me." I didn't know that, even though I was always present. We discussed strategies for addressing the behavior, and I kept a close eye on him afterward.

As children grow, they become more reluctant to share their feelings. Still, most children get chatty at bedtime. That's another natural moment to review the day, pray, and check whether anything is bothering them. When we pray, I always ask Willow to share her prayer requests. If I sense something is wrong and she isn't sharing, I'll ask, "Is there something you would like to change in your life right now?" This is a time for parents to practice patience and wait until our children are ready to share.

My friend's family goes around the dinner table each night to share their best and worst moments of the day. A single mom I know takes long walks with her teenage son, and they talk about the day. She says this is the only time her son opens up to her, and they have many rich conversations during these walks. A dad of four does a Saturday brunch every week with one child, creating precious one-on-one time in a full house.

Above all, stay encouraged and keep at it. Connection grows in small, steady moments of presence.

How can we show our children that we care?

We show interest by practicing intentional listening in small ways throughout the day. Even when we're preoccupied, when our child speaks, we can give them a moment of our full attention—pause, make eye contact, and listen. Then respond without irritation.

We ask their opinion on simple things, like what they want for dinner or what they want to do this weekend. These questions create mini-conversations.

We remember and follow up on topics that they introduce. How did the test go? How's the friend who was injured? Did the lost item turn up?

Before a connection drought sets in, we create rhythms and routines where talk is natural. This could be as simple as keeping cell phones off at dinner, or a weekly Sunday lunch out—just to talk. These habits create predictable, safe opportunities for our children to share and be heard. If we're already at a crisis point, start a new routine, and create a clear opening to talk.

I remember that when I was a kid, I would carefully consider what I told my parents and others. I'd rehearse a little speech and jot down the main points. I felt uncomfortable and unprepared when asked about a stressful or complex topic without time to think it through. As parents, we can offer advance notice for weighty conversations—"Let's talk after dinner; I'd love to hear your thoughts."

There are many subtle ways we can communicate our interest. When they talk to us, we should eliminate distractions. Turning off our phones in front of them communicates that we want to be fully present. When they address us, we look up right away rather than taking that extra few seconds to finish our email or text.

When a child confesses, that is sacred time. I withhold all punishment in these moments. I affirm my love for my daughter and that her honesty builds my trust. Once she admits wrongdoing, she is usually willing to talk about what happened and why. Then we discuss any consequences and how to respond. There are differing views on how to handle these moments. I desire that Willow will always confide in me, so I work hard to make sure she feels safe and secure when she does.

Few things matter more than seizing the moment when our children approach us, even if it's late, as they try to delay bedtime. If that is when they share and are most vulnerable, then that's the best time to listen and pray together.

How can we be better listeners?

Start by creating the right environment.

First, become aware of your current environment. Do you ever feel frazzled and realize that you're surrounded by chaos—the TV on, music blaring, everyone talking at once, things happening all around you? It can feel overwhelming and is not conducive to listening. If we choose what we let in and turn down distractions, we make a decisive move toward calm and peace. Then we can hear what's said and reflect on its meaning.

If you're in the center of activity and distracting noises, you might ask your child if you can talk in the next room. How wonderful to move—just the two of you—to a quiet space, kneel to their level (for some ages), and look them in the eye and wait in silence for them to share their heart. I often hold both my daughter's hands, put my arm around her, or pick her up. It shows I'm fully present and helps me avoid reaching for my phone.

Environment and place heighten our awareness of who is around us. Your child may not want others to hear their answer, or may need to talk about someone nearby. If your child isn't responding to your questions, it may help to ask, "Would you like to talk somewhere private?" If you're in public, you can slip out to the car for a moment together.

Choose the right time to listen. Listening can't be "squeezed" between meetings, right before school drop-off, or as you're hurrying out the door—those are classic hurry moments. But that might be the very moment your child decides to open up. Not convenient. When that happens, can you drop everything for a moment? Often, yes. We can reflect on what is more important right then—listening or being on time.

When I'm "on a mission," it's not easy for me to switch gears. I have to pause to reorient my focus. But listening to Willow in the moment and learning what upsets her is more important to me than the embarrassment of being late.

There are times when we can't drop everything. Even then, we can probably give our child our full attention long enough to communicate that we understand the importance of what they are saying; we want to listen and discuss it, but it's not possible right now. Then offer a time when we can reconnect. "Right after school," "after dinner on a walk," and "let's text for now" are simple options. We keep our word and follow up. Put it on the calendar, set an alarm—do what it takes so our children can rely on us.

Parents tell me their kids open up at the most inconvenient times—when it's past bedtime, when the parent is about to finish a long, complicated email, just as the family sits down for a favorite show. The most critical discussions happen at the most inconvenient times.

May I add that if you choose to listen to your child over your work, you don't have to apologize. A simple "I couldn't get here on time" is enough. The reason usually isn't the other person's business, and most don't ask for details. If sensitivity is needed, I say, "I really wanted to get here on time. I know this is important to you, and it's important to me, too. I'm sorry it wasn't possible to come earlier." **You never have to apologize for putting your child first.**

Waiting is critical. Once the place and time are right, and we've asked, "What's wrong?" or our child has raised a concern, *wait!* And wait some more if that's needed.

I struggle with waiting. It's unnatural for me. To help, I count in my head or intentionally slow my breathing and heart rate. Focusing my mind helps me be present.

Lately, I've added a simple practice. While I wait for the person I'm with to form their thoughts or gather the courage to open up, I look at them peacefully and patiently, and I pray in my heart, "Lord, make me quick to listen and slow to speak. Help this person I'm with find the right words." Prayer quiets my impulse to fix and frees me to hear. Patient listening becomes a meaningful act of love.

What does being present look like?

Being present is a journey. It is a slower pace of life. It's setting aside time for undivided attention to things that matter most. We choose what we let in and give our children our full attention. The key to being present is to find meaning in little moments as opportunities for us to connect with our children deeply, an investment in a lifelong relationship amid the hurry and noise.

Like everyone else, I find it difficult to be without my electronics. It takes effort to change a habit that's become second nature. We live in a world that often celebrates multitasking, time management, efficiency, and accomplishment. So I practice limits, and I'm learning to choose what I let in.

I tried to be present with Willow all the time, but honestly, when she was young, some of her activities were too boring for me. When I sat down to play with her, my mind started to list everything I "should" be doing—work, replying to emails, cleaning the fridge. Invariably, the washer or dishwasher would chime, and I would have more to do. I was distracted by my urge to check my phone, and I felt anxious being away from my laptop, as if I were "wasting time" while emails poured in. All I could hear was the sound of notifications going off in the background. But I knew, deep down, that all this was just a cultural drive I was conditioned to respond to.

When Willow was older, we would do puzzles and play games together. I loved it, and it was much easier for me than the toddler years. Still, being present took effort.

After practicing being present for years, I am grateful to see my growth. It's like strengthening a muscle. It was hard, but daily practice changed me. It now takes only a brief moment for me to get into our activity and focus on my daughter. Spending time with her feels so real. It feels fully human. I love it now. And more importantly, Willow feels loved.

We can move past our own preferences to prioritize the activities that our children enjoy most. As we learn to care more about being

together than the specific activity, we learn to enjoy being present—
and it becomes more natural.

How do we grow in patience?

Patience is tied to our sense of time. Consider how we view time—
and how our children experience it. In practice, impatience is often a
time problem: the tighter the clock, the shorter our tempers; the wider
the margins, the kinder our responses.

Have you tried to get a baby on a "schedule"? A newborn has
little sense of time beyond a basic internal clock that can be entirely off—sleeping during the day and staying awake all night. I was
often lectured on the need to plan my day and get Willow into my
routine. Truthfully, I thought it was ridiculous—I fed her when she
was hungry, and laid her down when she fell asleep. We got into a
natural rhythm, but it was flexible, just as I didn't always eat or sleep
at the same time. I decided to prioritize my new baby's personal
needs and rhythms over running the house according to a minute-
by-minute schedule. My heart broke to hear moms bragging about
how they never pick up their babies until 7:01 a.m.—"It doesn't
matter how loud they howl."

Some of you may picture my household as chaotic and wild.
The opposite is true. I have a peaceful home. As I respect my child's
natural rhythms, she senses and respects mine. On days when I
felt sick and needed to rest, my little toddler would climb onto the
bed beside me with a box of toys and play quietly until I got up.
This went against her high-energy nature, but I think children have
God-given intuition and sensitivity that we can develop if we are not
overly focused on enforcing a schedule.

A benefit of resisting rigid routines is that the child learns to be
adaptable and easygoing. It becomes okay to stay up late or go to
bed early when necessary. It becomes possible to go to evening
events and have more freedom.

So how does time connect to patience? When we are impatient with our children at any age, isn't it often because we are in a rush or trying to accomplish a great many things on a minute-by-minute schedule? We pressure ourselves to leave the home by exactly 7:50 a.m. or to pull into the church parking lot at 10:27 a.m. This creates immense pressure for children.

Just when we want to get out the door, our little ones want to do everything "by myself"—it feels like it takes forever. For older kids, we want them to listen and obey—we don't want everything to be an argument. We want them to hurry up and do what we ask without question or hesitation. Maybe we want to skip the whole "why" conversation and demand unquestioning obedience because we feel we have no time—team practice is starting soon. We are impatient.

When we loosen the pressure of time in low-stakes moments, we create space to be patient. Imagine if time were measured less precisely in daily life—if our commitments started at "about" noon or "around" three o'clock. What would happen? When the seconds and minutes don't matter so much, we become more patient because we are not concerned about being *a minute* late. We can choose to live with a more flexible routine and embrace spending that extra minute of quality time with our children. This isn't a case for chronic lateness; it's an invitation to build larger margins so love and spontaneity have room to act—a quiet resistance to busyness.

This perspective transformed my personal growth. When I'm in the greatest rush, pausing in that busy moment to wait patiently while a child gets her shoes on or grabs a favorite book or snack becomes a beautiful act of character formation. **In those pauses, I ask Christ to shine through my hurriedness as I choose to be patient and kind with my daughter and her friends.**

Admittedly, I am a by-the-minute person. I plan exactly when I want my family in our SUV, and my schedule is exact. If I had read this several years ago, I would have dismissed it as unrealistic, unattainable, and undesirable. But Willow is quite the opposite. She taught me that some things are much more important than being roughly on time. Countless times, I've had to turn the car around thirty seconds after leaving the driveway because Willow wanted to give her dad *one more* kiss goodbye. Willow is adamant—she asks, "What is more important—being on time or kissing my dad?" Honestly, I think being on time!

So I've had to change. Being patient in my context means allowing ourselves to be five minutes "late." I find it stressful to be late, so I now plan to be at the door fifteen minutes before we need to leave. There is time for "I just have to get something." I anticipate last-minute delays, and I've planned for them. I can embrace being *more or less* on time rather than early. I can patiently stand at the door and know that I'll still be on time. And if I am not on time, I remind myself that it doesn't matter in the grand scheme.

That gets to the heart of patience. What matters most? Being on time and meeting others' expectations, or letting our children do things themselves, and responding kindly when they realize in the car that they have to go back into the house to use the restroom?

In the big picture of life, what is more important: rushing through this moment of learning and discovering or taking the time to teach your child something new? Should we demand that they do what we ask and brush off their questions, objections, and concerns, or should we take the time to remind our children of our values and discuss them when the opportunity presents itself? With older children, we know that these moments can be rare.

Life goes by far too quickly. At the end of our days, being on time will have no lasting meaning. **Choosing to set the clock aside so we can truly live life with our children—that is what matters. Those precious moments slow down the racing clock of life by creating a life full of meaning and sweet memories.**

Which habits erode a child's trust?

The qualities that make for great parenting have unhealthy flip sides.

We've talked about the importance of patience. Impatience is corrosive. It shows up as screaming at children, losing control of our words, and resorting to cursing, insulting, mocking, or making fun of their weaknesses. Whether impulsive or deliberate, these patterns humiliate a child and dismantle trust—often without parents realizing the damage as it happens in real time.

Likewise, many parents subtly disrespect their children—interrupting, dismissing their comments and questions, labeling their emotions as "overly dramatic" or "crazy," excusing hurtful statements by saying we didn't mean them—we were just tired or joking—and disregarding their personal possessions and space.

We have inherent authority as parents, but we can unconsciously misuse it. Our authority should never imply that our children's opinions aren't valid. Sometimes children use the wrong terms or struggle to describe what they really mean, so we should avoid interrupting, finishing their sentences, or rewording their statements. When they make a mistake, we can pause before we correct them; we can give them time to self-correct.

Our children may especially value words or time spent together. If so, we should give *extra* attention to the words we use and the time we spend with them. When words and time make them feel loved most, insults and being ignored are all the more hurtful.

We can surrender our destructive habits to God. We can pray for healing where we have caused pain to our children, redemption where we have broken trust, and love to move forward in grace. As God leads us, we can confess, apologize, and practice small, consistent changes that rebuild trust over time.

How can we avoid common parenting pitfalls?

Observing our children's personalities and responding appropriately as they grow and develop is essential; it is one way we value and respect them. I had to learn to be careful and respect Willow's possessions. I don't understand why she treasures little trinkets; I am inclined to consider them "junk" and throw them away. However, whenever I've done so, it upset her, and I regretted it. So I have discovered that honoring Willow means helping her keep her many mementos organized—and not purging her old toys without her permission.

We curb hurtful habits by mindfully managing our voice and tone. There are times when I've caught myself using a soft, sweet tone with Willow's friends, but a sharp, harsh tone with my own daughter. It breaks my heart to admit this. I sounded much more empathetic toward the other child. Willow picked up on it. Thankfully, she is forgiving, and we discussed it thoroughly, and I apologized in detail, acknowledging that I hadn't been kind or fair to her.

We may have a habit of putting down our children in front of others. That's humiliating for them. We don't need to share our children's personal shortcomings, struggles, and weaknesses with others. We don't need to insult them, make fun of them, or talk about how this or that habit or stage is so frustrating to us when they are within earshot.

Instead, create the opposite habit. We can stop ourselves from putting down our children and use the opportunity to build them up in front of others. What a difference it makes. Let's celebrate our children within their hearing, affirming them, and saying we love them. Imagine how our children will feel if they *overhear* us speaking proudly about how wonderful they are and how much we love them, rather than airing their faults.

This is a powerful way to communicate our adoration for older children. There's an assumption that parents say they love their kids to their faces because it's expected and easy. But I find that hearing Mom and Dad boast about their children in front of others—and talk about how much they love them within earshot—is deeply affirming to children of all ages.

In short, we can ensure that our children know we hear and see them, that we care about their feelings, value their opinions and perspectives, and love them unconditionally—that our love is not contingent on their obedience or any other actions. There are wise times and methods to offer correction, but disparaging children in public to make a point is not healthy. Even when it happens at home, it is unnecessary and counterproductive.

Thankfully, whatever mistakes we have made, we can turn around. By God's grace, we can reset the atmosphere of the home. We can choose to speak words of life and affirmation over our children. We can show love and affection at all times. We can build them up in private and in public, reminding them of all the things we love about them. When these conscious, constructive habits become part of our daily rhythm, we position our children to flourish, catching a glimpse of their heavenly Father through our example—loving, trustworthy, kind, and affirming.

What helps when we're angry?

Sadly, we've all witnessed a parent ripping into a child over a small matter and shuddered at the hurt in the child's eyes. We don't want to respond like that.

It helps to identify early indicators. When we're angry or frustrated, our first instinct may be to yell. When we feel this urge, we can step away for a few seconds or remain silent for a moment to calm down before reacting. This pause gives us a moment to consider the best response and whether the situation warrants our anger. We can watch our tone and volume. When we hear ourself raising our voice, we can take a deep breath.

That adage about silently counting to ten works well—it allows us to focus our breathing and slow our heart rate, and ten seconds later, we feel calmer. Once we're calm, we can speak slowly and carefully.

Later, we bring the situation to God in prayer. We try to understand what made us angry and surrender it to God. If there is an underlying issue, we may need to "talk it out" with our spouse or friend. Sometimes we may realize that our child was simply mirroring our actions—and we can commit to doing better.

The hardest part may be apologizing; it requires humility. My instinct is to blame my daughter for "making" me angry. If a drink spills and leaves me with a mess to clean up, I can blame Willow for my frustration. But an angry response does more harm than an accidental spill. I need to ask forgiveness when my response isn't a reflection of God's love.

With time, this process becomes second nature. We can catch ourselves before we raise our voices and be quick to apologize when we do.

When we lead in kindness, our children learn to control their anger, and forgiveness becomes a natural response in our homes. I see this maturity in Willow—she quickly forgives and offers her own apology, perhaps for not being careful. It's a loving, tender moment.

Above all, we can try not to make others the recipients of our anger. The world today can feel like an angry place. It seems acceptable to harbor deep anger, act on it, and feel justified. But this does not produce good fruit—especially when busyness has already frayed everyone's nerves.

God helps us respond with love rather than hurting the people we love most. **God is love. We can ask for wisdom, patience, and self-control in the moment—and the courage to repair afterward.** We confess, apologize, and try again. Our gracious responses model kindness to our children, who grow to trust us and see God as loving and forgiving, too.

How can we find contentment and fulfillment as parents?

The greatest challenge I face as a parent is feeling lonely and restless. I often feel guilty because I have a wonderful daughter, husband, and good friends; I am deeply blessed, yet I still yearn for more.

We can pray that God helps us to live out the reality that God is enough. Our family is enough. We are enough.

When I was younger, I found my excitement for life centered on church activities and community—that was helpful. Now, I strive to focus on God's presence in my home, which is even better. God is here. With me. Guiding me and giving my days meaning.

When this comes into focus, we see our family in a whole new light. We can be happy and fulfilled at home with our family when we center our lives on Christ.

This perspective doesn't yet come naturally to me, but I am learning to remind myself daily to find meaning and comfort in my family and in God's presence right here. This brings me peace and joy, easing my loneliness.

What if the most sacred sanctuary of God's presence in our lives is our own home? What if our home is the place we are most aware of God moving in our lives? What if our best self comes to life right here?

When we create a home where God is central and we are a conduit of God's love to our family, our hearts return to gratitude, and we feel a deeper sense of meaning and fulfillment.

Sometimes when I have a hard day, I let Willow watch a show while I call a friend to connect—and that's okay.

Home can be holy ground—God is enough, and so are we.

How do we build connections and mend broken relationships?

Meaningful relationships grow as we sacrifice our wants and love unconditionally. God often mends relationships through sacrificial love and slow, faithful presence.

Does creating a strong relationship with our children matter most to us? Sometimes the honest answer is no. What do we ultimately desire most—time on our devices, achievements, the rush of multitasking, efficiency wins—or time with our children? What gives us the most satisfaction for the long haul, not just the moment?

For parents with children who can't yet communicate verbally, or for those with older kids who retreat into their own worlds, you may prefer to be alone with your device rather than do the hard work of reengaging a little one or drawing out an older child. You may feel distant from your children and wonder where to start to rebuild a broken relationship. Spending time with a child who doesn't look up from a screen to acknowledge you can feel wasted.

I feel sorrow alongside you because that is a hard place to be. It can leave you feeling like your love for your child is one-way, with you giving yourself but receiving rejection in return. Maybe you fear that your best efforts to create quality time with your children will ultimately fail. It's frustrating and disappointing.

If we want a close relationship with our children, even if it takes years of investment, we must keep trying. The alternative is letting the broader culture shape them for us.

So what can we do to keep moving forward? First, we find encouragement in the Lord and in friends who will walk with us and pray for us. We must keep reminding ourselves of what matters most—investing in our children. Even when we don't see any immediate visible response or tangible results, we must believe we are making an investment in their future and their relationship with God. **We are making an impact far beyond what we can see today.**

Without a doubt, it will require great patience and trust in God. Our resistance against the culture of isolation and broken relationships will not be easy. When relational distance discourages us, we can keep showing up with God's help—choosing to stay connected even when it's hard.

How can we create environments that help children focus and flourish?

When we tap into a child's personality and what brings them joy, we can make activities more engaging.

Willow struggled to complete her phonics lessons. Bored by some sections, she found endless ways to delay. It took too long to finish her lesson—and tested my patience. One night, as Willow was falling asleep, she curled up beside me and sleepily said, "Mom, please don't go until I'm asleep. I love your cuddles." The next day, I suggested a new place to do phonics—not at the dining room table on hard chairs, but cuddled together on our oversized lounge chair. It worked. We went through the lesson with no interruptions. I kept an arm around her the whole time, and she could stay cuddled while learning to read. She loved it.

What a shift. Willow was happy to do an activity she hadn't been fond of because it also meant cuddle time, and she got my undivided attention.

Years later, I couldn't get Willow to practice the piano at home—until I realized I was sending her downstairs, apart from me. We moved the keyboard to the main level, and I sat beside her; right away, we got into a daily rhythm that became enjoyable.

That's the difference when we tap into a child's personality to see what works for them. I remind myself that it's not wasted time. It's time together. Being attentive to a child's personality and creating the dynamics that fit will help them flourish.

A child's environment matters. My friend complained that her ten-year-old would not stay seated at his desk for more than a short moment. I found his desk in a nook beside the kitchen, facing a marked-up white wall. There were no windows in view. The space was devoid of color and anything enlivening. The desk chair was hardwood with a straight back and a flat seat; his knees bent too sharply and hit the desk when he sat. In other words, the space was uncomfortable, uncreative, uninspiring, and noisy. None of us would choose such a place to work or learn.

To help our children flourish, we can create a beautiful space. Comfortable, inviting, inspiring. We can position our children's desks to face a window, allowing them to enjoy the natural light and the welcome momentary distraction of birds, squirrels, trees, sky, and space that lifts the heart. Together, plant favorite flowers and set up birdhouses within view. Find a place away from the noise and busy-ness of the kitchen, yet near us. Hang beautiful art that inspires. Let younger children set up a favorite stuffed animal by their chair. Have the older children choose their own lamp and décor theme. Maybe add a cozy chair and a soft rug.

Some children get overwhelmed or distracted by a cluttered space. A helpful pre-study routine is to take a minute or two to tidy the space. Once a week, provide a more thorough tidying to ensure everything has a designated place and is properly organized and dust-free.

Consider the light and air quality, as well as the level of noise and activity in their space. Bright, fluorescent lighting, especially when accompanied by a high-pitched hum, is not helpful. We can work to eliminate unnecessary noises (including those from our own devices), distractions, and temptations that make it harder to focus in that space.

When Willow is busy with an activity, I avoid tasks that create loud noises. I set my phone to silent and try not to be *busy* around her. I don't interrupt her. I also don't instruct her—if she has a question or needs help, she will ask. Review and correction come later, when she's ready for me to look over her work.

Leave out something new—like a book or craft—to spark your child's interest. Set out quality art supplies. When we show interest in an activity, our children are more likely to join us.

We all grow in our ability to focus over time. Stay encouraged. It helps to remind Willow of the natural consequences when she delays—we won't leave for an outing until her homework is done; friends don't come over unless her room is tidy. Our family rule is that once we start a project, we try to finish it—and "leave no evidence." This applies to me, too—if I am folding laundry and she wants something, she can wait a couple of minutes until I am finished. Best of all, if she is in a rush, she can help me.

What rhythms help children keep their spaces tidy?

Here are several routines to maintain consistently clean and tidy children's spaces at home.

A basic need is **good organization**. Does everything have a place, or do we need to reorganize a bit? Are any containers jam-packed? If so, what can we pass on to another child? Are there items children aren't using that we can rotate out for a time and bring back later? Can children easily access containers, reach shelves, and use the organization system?

Children may need help finding a place for new items when they come home. Open, clear containers on shelves with room to spare work best for us, so matching items can be quickly tossed in.

The next step is maintenance—**clean-room check-ins** anchored to natural moments in the day. In our home, that's after breakfast (make the bed, open the curtains, put away last night's clothes), late afternoon (tidy the day's activities), and a late-night check (put away evening activities).

As long as there are only a few items, most children can tidy up on their own. When a check-in is missed or friends visit, the clutter adds up, and children can feel overwhelmed or unsure where to start.

Several approaches are simple and break up the task so children can see **steady progress**—a limited number (do two or five or ten things, then repeat), a limited time (tidy for just five minutes; take a short break; return for five minutes), and spatial progress (start at the door or in a corner and move forward, tidying whatever item appears next). The third option is not as efficient, but the results are immediate and encourage a child to keep going.

If help is needed, pair up and aim for equal effort—each person does ten things.

When motivation dips, try a contest or race. Give one clear instruction at a time—"gather the LEGO bricks," then "shelve the books." Am I too busy with my own list to help in the moment? I'll try to stack tasks: "Put three things away while I vacuum the kitchen," then "Now put away all the doll accessories while I send an email—let's see who finishes first."

One item at a time, the job gets done.

Consequences are a lifeline. We link privileges to readiness—playdates or outings follow a clean room. If time is short, I'll help while explaining that I am happy to show kindness, but our goal is for each person to care for their own space so our home thrives and we have time to connect in joyful ways.

How can we navigate negative influences from friends?

Most parents see how quickly kids mimic peers and test their newfound behaviors at home.

Open communication with our children is a helpful response. Conversations can turn negative behaviors into opportunities to discuss our values together.

I remember the first time Willow said, "That boy is not nice. I don't want to play with him." She got it. She recognized that his behavior—hitting other children—was not acceptable, and she did not want to be around that influence.

But kids need friends. I didn't want her to become antisocial and lonely. Gradually, she learned to live alongside different values—staying connected without being overly shaped by them.

If we are faith-filled parents, we hope our children will be a light to others and examples of God's love. So we can't run away from every misbehaving child. We can discuss their friends regularly and ask questions. We can talk about any behaviors and words that upset our children. We can review how to be a good example to others with kind, clear boundaries. Over time, this strengthens their resistance to negative influences and their ability to model kindness within clear limits.

This approach applies to older children as well. We begin by asking questions; then we listen to our child's perspective. There are likely factors in the situation that we don't know about, so we listen carefully and discuss them together.

Then we come to the difficult decision of whether to ask our children to avoid a negative influence for a while, or to find ways they can be a light to a troubled child. We can ask our child: "Are you comfortable making a positive impact on this friend, or do you feel the friendship needs space?" To the extent that we can monitor the situation, and it's safe and wise, we can support our children as they stand firm and influence their friends for good. We can role-play so that our children are comfortable saying no and articulating why.

Parenting requires wisdom. We can create space between our kids and friends who present unhealthy situations, and we can guide our children to resist unhelpful influence and to be witnesses of God's love.

The short answer is "Pray, pray, and pray some more." Keep the lines of communication open with our children so they can learn and grow, and so we learn from them and about them. With God's help, our steady conversation and small, kind boundaries help keep influence flowing the right way.

How do we protect our kids' privacy when we post?

Privacy is a major concern: we have limited control over our children's information once it's online. Institutions and platforms collect data in ways we rarely see, and even friends and family may share photos and information about our children online without our knowledge or consent.

We can be mindful and respectful of our children's privacy from day one—even before day one, during pregnancy or adoption—and we can consider the potential future impact of what we share. Reflect on questions like these:

- What is the impact of publicly posting hundreds of photos of our children?
- Is it wise to create social media profiles for them before they can consent?

- How might our children feel about today's posts years from now, especially ones that share intimate details of their lives?
- Could our public complaints about parenting—or about our children—hurt them when they are old enough to view what we've posted?
- Should strangers have access to information about our children's health, personality, activities, and home life?

A helpful filter is to consider how our children might feel about what we've shared—and how others might use it to harm or shame them. Ask your child how they feel about you sharing a story, photo, or video about them.

A common pushback is that social media is a tool to communicate with family. I agree. I've sent hundreds of photos and videos to family members who live far away—privately.

Social media is a powerful tool for communicating, yet it can also intrude on privacy. Remember that everything we post, like, and share is analyzed and stored by the platforms we use.

There are risks associated with posting photos of our children online. It is wise to research who holds the data, how long it is retained, and what controls we have.

Teach your children about privacy and the importance of celebrating life in person, not just through online communication. Talk about how real life differs from online life.

Many young people have never known a world without social media and may lack healthy privacy boundaries; we can model good boundaries. We honor our children's humanity by letting them shape their own identity and share it when they're ready.

When our family celebrates or has a funny moment, I encourage Willow to call her grandparents and tell them herself—strengthening relationships and growing her storytelling skills. It also gives me insight into what she's comfortable sharing and how she frames the moment for others.

Before we post, remember that privacy is sacred. Pause to pray, "God, should I share this?" and consider how your child will feel now and later. **If you hesitate at all, don't post.**

Should we be concerned about advertising?

Privacy and protecting our children from the influence of advertising are closely connected. Ads are invasive—entering our homes unwelcome and often hyper-targeted.

They also teach and model values for our children.

For example, do your social media apps ever showcase short videos that frame cellulite or a soft belly as undesirable? How might such messages shape a child's sense of worth, body image, and understanding of natural aging?

Ads too often oppose our values. When those messages are delivered into private spaces—and tailored by data collected about us—they become both a privacy concern and a formative force that may not align with our faith and identity in God.

How do we help our children avoid the influence of ads?

Ads are everywhere—they can feel inescapable. As adults, we often learn to ignore them, but children can feel overwhelmed. The content may raise concerns and questions that are not age-appropriate. In my experience, ads rob us of peace.

There are ways we can reduce exposure.

At restaurants, I position Willow as far away from the TVs as possible. She usually sits beside me, so I am deliberate about which seat I choose. I won't take a booth too close to a screen. Some restaurants have individual TVs at each booth. If the host can't turn it off for us, we ask to sit elsewhere.

Billboards, bus ads, and streaming ads are the hardest to avoid. When I see certain ones, I pray Willow doesn't notice them. If she comments or asks questions, my husband and I do our best to respond by affirming our values and explaining what we don't like about the ad's message.

By design, product ads prompt a child to want more and more stuff. We can keep reminding our children to be thankful for all that God has given them, and to fix our minds on being grateful, and to learn not to desire every new product we see.

We can partially control the direct advertising that enters our homes by blocking electronic ads. Some mobile phone apps have a monthly fee, but we can search for free options too. The same applies to some streaming apps.

As much as we can, we try to have a logo-free home. I can't escape the logo on my phone, but I cover it with a case. I cover the logo on my laptop with a sticker. We avoid clothes with bold brand names pasted on the front.

Why does it matter? It minimizes the commercial side of our world and turns our attention back to the natural world. To this end, we have plants, nature images, and real wood around us whenever possible. We use clay mugs for our morning coffee. These are small acts to improve our healthy relationship with God's natural world.

We all stumble as parents. With humility, prayer, and God's help, our small faithful choices—to listen, to be present, to practice patience, to apologize when our actions wound, and to build wise boundaries—help us stay connected amid hurry, noise, and busyness and keep drawing our hearts back together.

Reflection

1. Which listening habits will you practice this week (eye contact, no interrupting, follow-up questions)? Write three specific dinner table questions you'll ask tonight to learn about your family's day—and help you stay connected.

2. How can you build a deeper connection with each family member? What daily routine can you start to create space for meaningful conversations amid the busyness?

3. Is there a relationship that needs mending? Take one step toward forgiveness, and begin nurturing a better connection.

4. What habits can you begin to build to grow in greater patience? What are your anger "early indicators," and what habits can you practice (count to ten, step away, breathe, pray) to pause and reset when hurry and noise creep in?

5. Define your family's privacy rule for posting about your children. How will you model this? How will you communicate this to relatives and friends?

6. How can you reduce the influence of negative messaging from ads in your home (ad-free apps, browser/ad blockers, mute/skip ads)? Pick one to implement this week.

Family Conversation Starters

- "What habits can we nurture to listen better to one another? What can we say to each other when we feel we are not being listened to, so we can stay connected?"
- "What does patience look like? What helps us be patient? What does anger look like? How can we pause when we start to feel angry?"
- "When friends pressure us to break a family rule, how should we respond?"
- "Let's talk about our study space, play space, and sleep space. Do they feel peaceful? What simple changes (lighting, chair, view, clutter, supplies) would help us focus and feel more peaceful there?"

Rhythms for This Week

1. Note the times in your daily routines that can be sacred moments to connect—while driving, at dinner, or before bedtime—simple anchors for staying connected.

2. Identify one interest for each family member. Take a step toward bonding with them over that interest.

3. Choose one habit—say, to be more present or less angry—and note how you can work on it.

---

4. List ways to adjust your home environment to cultivate peace and joy. Create a simple plan to put them in place.

Part Four

AN INVITATION

Choosing loving connection, joy, and peace

Seven

MAKING EVERYDAY FAITH YOURS

SAY YES TO loving connection, joy, and peace!

You can live by your values and lead your family—one small, faithful step at a time.

You're here because these stories stirred in you a desire for more for your family. As you read this final chapter, be encouraged to turn values into everyday rhythms so your home grows in connection, joy, and peace.

You'll find simple practices you can adapt for your season—tools to help you lead with faith-based, family-centered values. Take them one by one, asking God where to begin.

Trust that God will graciously supply what you need for each small step toward a more loving, faith-filled, family-centered home.

Steps to build new rhythms and a new way of life

You might wonder if it's possible to create a whole new way of life for your family. Be encouraged—change is possible. It takes time, effort, and perseverance; wisdom seeks strength and help from God every day.

Here's what has helped us.

Humility. First, I admit that I am often part of the problem. There are days when I want to zone out. I choose my phone over giving attention to my family.

I have to admit this if I am to change our family culture. Change is hard. I don't want to admit it—or to change. I resist using my phone less—with a hundred excuses for why I "need" it as a professional serving our clients.

I name the truth of how I feel; then I confess the reality of the challenge before me. Next, I remind myself of the greater rewards of the changes I seek and of being present with my family.

Humility is also essential when we ask for feedback from our family. One of the toughest yet most rewarding questions I ask my husband is "What can I do to build a happier relationship with you?"

If he says that a tidier house would be more peaceful for him, I immediately think, *The house is perfectly fine! Doesn't he know how hard I work? How can he think that I could add more to my life?* Or when he says he's frustrated that I always need the last word, my head explodes with counterarguments. Isn't it human nature to react with pride?

However, Larry's responses have led me to significant self-awareness and personal growth. I've been able to improve our family life in many ways after talking with him. For example, with Willow's stuff creating too much clutter, Larry worked with me to create a better-organized space for her items, took more initiative to remind her to put her things away during the day, and lowered his expectations of tidiness—a win for me!

So I admit I dread asking Larry how I can improve; my first response is always to get defensive and argue in my head. Still, when I humbly accept his loving criticism, discuss what he means, and work on a solution together, our family life flourishes.

Humility is an essential aspect of creating positive change in a family.

Communication. Begin by sharing your desire for positive change with all family members. Tell your kids that you wish to spend more time with them. You want to know them better. You want to do more fun things together and create special memories that cultivate joy and connection.

Ask them what they think. Ask them what they would like from you and from each other. Then wait. *Wait*. Let silence be your friend. Give them time to think and answer.

Let them contribute ideas about what a better future for your family could look like.

Then leave the topic for them to consider. At a later time, restate what you would like to see for your family and from them. Again, get feedback. Keep listening.

It may take the children several days to process what would make family life happier from their perspective.

In my experience, the next best step is to start with ourselves. Ask your family, "What would you like me to do to bring positive change in our home? How can I be more present in your life? What can I do to strengthen our relationships?"

Then pause. Listen to their ideas. Receive what they share with humility. Choose not to be offended or to argue if they offer criticism, express hurt, or even make accusations as they describe what quality time with you could look like.

Gradually work toward what they ask for, and invite the family to join you in the quest. For example, all family members could agree to keep their devices silent and out of sight during mealtimes. Maybe everyone could spend an hour every night together, with all devices turned off to safeguard peace and nurture connection.

One day, Willow got upset at me for "always talking on the phone." We agreed that I would shut off the notification sounds, though I left my ringer on. Our home is more peaceful without dings and beeps from my phone. When I check for messages, it is at my convenience,

131

not "on demand" from a sound. Those who know me well call if they have an urgent message.

We then discussed my need to get work done during the day, including while I'm spending time with her. She offered that I could ask her "permission" before making a call, and then she wouldn't mind. At the time, she was three years old. I wasn't sure she understood the term "permission," and I was certain this plan would end poorly. But it didn't! Her system works well, and we have used it for years.

I still ask if she minds my making a call. Almost always, she says, "Sure." Sometimes she asks how long it will be, and occasionally, when I thoughtlessly ask to make a call while we're having fun, she says she really doesn't want me to be on the phone until after our activity. I've come to appreciate her honesty, and this arrangement has eliminated her sense that I was *always* on my phone.

In some homes, parents decide all the family rules. For me, inviting Willow into the discussion and explaining how much it means to me works much better.

Give it to God. Often! Let's commit all our ways to God. Certainly, we can commit to God something as crucial as building better relationships with our family members. God is faithful. And praying as a family for God's help is a great step toward growing closer together in connection, joy, and peace.

Acknowledge the challenge of change

Making values-driven family decisions often feels countercultural. It's a round-the-clock challenge—kids accustomed to constant electronics may ask for them again and again. We may see big feelings— protests, tears, and anger—when we put devices away and turn off the TV as new habits take root. Acknowledging these challenges from the outset helps us reckon with the weight of our decision and its implications for everyday faith at home.

A friend once encouraged me: **I don't need to be supermom; I just need to be a little stronger than my daughter.** It turned out to be true!

Willow has her days when she is insistent and relentless. Those are tough days. She also has days when one reminder is enough, and she responds with a joyful attitude. To my delight, there are days when she does things for me without even being asked! Hard to believe, but sometimes she pulls out the vacuum simply because she sees a mess and figures she can clean it up herself. I run over to see what's *wrong*. Then I realize Willow is beginning to understand what it means to be part of our family. Something is clicking. She is getting it. I'm reminded that not everything is a battle.

The rewards of a life that is coherent, consistent, and aligned with our family's values are worth all the effort and struggle.

As children practice new rhythms, they learn to lead in small ways, and those small acts begin to model shared values to others.

Invite kids to lead

Do you want your children to follow or lead? Blend in or stand for their values and reflect the love of Jesus?

Let's call them to lead—to carry your family values into real moments with kindness and courage, free from the pressure to chase cultural trends so their everyday faith becomes visible.

The impact can be incredible.

You'll begin to see a transformation in the way your children think. Instead of angry responses, they start to understand the reasoning behind your family rules. They begin to take ownership of those rules and share family values with friends in ways that build connection and joy.

In our home, Willow learned that when friends visit, we invest in meaningful time together. We want to create memories, so we don't watch TV or movies. When new friends ask to watch, I hear Willow say, "At our house, we don't do screens when friends are over, but we can ask my mom to set up a craft or a game." She came up with the idea of hiding her electronics in a closet when friends are coming to reduce temptation. Willow has learned we're a values-driven family, and she now influences others by confidently sharing our values. That's leadership.

Over time, our friends realized we do other activities—arts and crafts, games, and playing outside. They came to love it. The little ones would burst through the door, asking what we were going to do today. The older kids would arrive with a favorite game already in mind.

Leadership is broad. Not every child is comfortable speaking up. One of Willow's friends leads quietly. She loves water activities, and when Willow kept saying no, her friend simply put on her bathing suit and began to play. Her calm example drew the others in—soon, all the kids were playing water activities with her. That's leadership too. Willow's friend is quiet and peaceful, but her leadership in these moments led the kids to follow her example.

In both of these examples, I didn't have to lecture or correct.

This approach helps children live out faith and family values. Parents share the work of weaving values into daily life, and everyone has a role. When you release your kids to lead in small ways, your home culture strengthens—and your values show up in their choices long after you leave the room as the fruit of everyday faith.

Commit wholeheartedly

Commit to your values wholeheartedly—without compromise—and live them consistently.

Wholehearted commitment makes life *easier* by giving you a simple, solid framework for your actions, words, and decisions—particularly on busy days when peace and connection are tested.

Of course, your commitment begins with you. As you live out your values day after day, you can be confident that your children will follow your lead over time.

When I feel overwhelmed by the many negative influences on our children—and there are many—I remember that **my husband and I are the greatest influence on our daughter.**

What I say, how I say it, and what I do speak volumes to Willow. Children are always watching and learning from us; the example we set can guide them for the rest of their lives.

This brings me great comfort because I can govern my own words and actions—I can steward the greatest influence in my daughter's life.

Plan for change

Have a plan. Stick to it.

If your kids are overly reliant on screens and struggle when they're removed, how can you help them overcome this dependence? You need a plan for how you'll respond and what will replace screen-based entertainment so joy, peace, and connection can flourish.

Preplanning for my toddler meant keeping the lower shelves of a linen closet stocked with engaging activities, puzzles, and craft supplies. We kept her playroom organized and clean, so she wanted to spend time there and discover new interests. We rotated her toys. When I found her toddler activities boring, fresh options helped keep us both engaged.

For older kids, tap into their existing interests. Perhaps they have no hands-on interests or hobbies. Ask what they enjoy most on their screens and start there. Do they love dance shows? Car racing games? What can you do in the real world that engages those interests?

The financial investment in activities for older children is higher. But deals can still be found at thrift stores and online marketplaces. Securing the funds can be a learning experience—what ideas does your teenager have for raising the funds and sourcing inexpensive options?

As parents, set the tone for new activities. "Let's go for a family walk." "Let's make a new recipe for your favorite dish." Do you need to reorganize a closet? Do it together—and let your child take the lead. Maybe your child has great ideas for organizing! Or they may create a brand-new dish or discover a new, off-the-beaten-path place for a hike.

Find ways to be fully present in the moment. Train your mind not to slip away to check your phone so connection stays front and center.

Create new ways together

Moving toward less screen time and more real-life experiences that reflect our values each day won't be easy. I stay motivated by remembering that I want Willow to make a meaningful difference in the world and to be a leader. I need to practice leadership with her today so she's equipped to resist peer and cultural pressures tomorrow—and live out everyday faith.

Take time to talk as a family every day. When your values collide with what your children are learning or unconsciously picking up from other kids, treat those moments as opportunities to teach your children to stand for what they believe, to lead, to set an example, and to make a gentle impact on their friends' lives. It starts with intentionality.

Most important? Commit all your ways and all your days to God in prayer. Every morning (set an alarm if needed), commit your family, your words, and your actions to God and ask the Lord to empower you to be a living example of godly love to your children. Interceding privately for your children is a powerful way for God to change your heart and help you grow in love and patience for your kids.

Give yourself grace. **Receive God's forgiveness for past missteps.** In accepting God's forgiveness, you set an example for your children to forgive you and to forgive themselves.

Trust that the seeds you are planting will bear fruit in their lives in the days to come—in God's time and in ways you may not see right away.

Make the change

With God, anything is possible.

I know this because I have become a new person. I transformed from a car-wreck survivor and new mom struggling with low self-confidence to a woman strengthened by the Lord, and a mom who unashamedly leads my child on a countercultural path of honoring God, family, and healthy living with everyday faith guiding our steps.

I have struggled with screen overuse, fear, anxiety, depression, and loneliness, to name a few battles I've faced.

When I came to the end of myself as an exhausted mom unable to live up to the standards I had set for myself, I surrendered fully to God. In that moment, in my weakness, I discovered the sustaining power of living by God's strength.

We always have a reason to hope. **God is here for us, steadily working right alongside us.** We have a profound influence on our children, regardless of their age. The greatest change we can make in our children is the change we make in ourselves. We keep striving to live the example we want them to follow. The way we live our daily lives is our loudest lesson.

Let's start by being present: turn off electronics and everything that buzzes, put devices out of sight, and be fully present with our children.

This is a path to finding meaning and purpose for our lives. It's about doing the things that truly matter—investing in the lives of the people we love most and, in turn, creating rich memories full of joy and wonder, moments that matter and knit connection.

Resist cultural voices that pressure us to conform and compromise our values—voices that push us to be ordinary. Instead, let's go for all God calls us to be. Let's follow our convictions and values. Let's have a higher vision for our families than the broken disconnectedness we see around us. It is a call to be courageous and countercultural!

Cultivate the fruit of the Spirit—"love, joy, peace, patience, kindness, goodness, faithfulness, gentleness, self-control" (see Galatians 5:22–23). Above all, let's be patient. If we practice patience, we are more likely to avoid the outbursts that lead to hurt and rejection.

Faith is our sure foundation. It gives purpose and offers our children an anchor when we are not with them. Teaching God's truth is one of the hardest tasks because we embody the message we teach. We are called to speak words of life, truth, and affirmation over our children and to demonstrate God's love at every opportunity so that our everyday faith becomes the tone of our home.

If we do this, if we live out God's calling as parents, we position our family for a transformation from the emptiness of modern culture to the fullness of connectedness, order, meaningful relationships, and purpose. This is countercultural parenting—and by God's grace, it is possible.

Hear God in the everyday

Keeping God's Word at the center of my life helps me become the parent I long to be. Meditating on Scripture shapes my character.

Patience is a significant theme in this book, and that stems from my own growth in this area. Early on, I made *practicing patience* my New Year's resolution. It took two years before I felt I had made enough progress to move on to joy, followed by love, then kindness. I'm now working on peace. One by one, the fruit of the Spirit took shape within me as I meditated on Scripture—and that transformed my relationship with my husband and daughter.

In busy seasons, I kept it simple. When I felt too overwhelmed to sit and read Scripture, God graciously met me through worship songs, Sunday sermons, friends with timely words of encouragement, and His peaceful presence.

Thankfully, hard seasons pass, and you can **rebuild rhythms that include Scripture**. This can take different forms—audio Bibles and podcasts on the go, a Bible study with friends, or a daily devotional when you are solo. You can study Scripture as a family after meals, while driving, or before bedtime. My university students introduced me to verse-a-day apps so that not a single day passes without a word of Scripture.

Devotional books can help you go deeper into a passage. Start with the *Women in the Bible* study and video series I published.[2] For moms, look up Sandee Macgregor's devotional books for mothers to do with their children.[3]

Once we establish routines that include Scripture, **how do we discern God's voice?**

As you read Scripture, pause when your heart is stirred by a verse or word, or when the passage seems to relate to your situation. Reflect on how it relates to you and your family. Write out what it means in a journal or discuss it with a friend, and then pray about it. This helps you internalize and remember what God has laid on your heart.

Simple questions help us reflect on Scripture:

- Which verses stand out to you in this passage?
- What inspires or challenges you from these verses—and why?
- How can you apply today's wisdom to your life and family?

Over time, you learn to recognize God's guidance. God prompts our hearts and minds toward obedience and spiritual growth, giving us wisdom for each challenge on our journey.

For me, God's guidance often comes through a song that re-centers me on God and His promises or through a friend's loving advice or encouragement. I then reflect on it: Does the prompting align with Scripture and the character of Jesus? Does it bear the fruit of the Spirit within me? How should I respond?

---

2. *Women in the Bible Small Group Bible Study* (Castle Quay Books) presents an eight-week study of women in the Bible for personal and small group use with accompanying videos.

3. See Sandee Macgregor's *A Mother-Daughter Devotional and Shared Journal Experience for Psalm 119* and *A Devotional for Mothers and Sons: Walking in Wisdom Through Proverbs* (Castle Quay Books).

Peace, joy, and loving-kindness at home are possible—with God's help. Change comes as we walk with God in the ordinary—one verse, one prayer, one small step at a time. Over time, values become rhythms that shape a faith-centered home.

Fulfill your calling

Remember: God has chosen you to be a parent! You may feel lonely, but you are not alone. God is with you and guiding you.

There will be hard moments and difficult days, but God will equip you every step of the way. You may feel inadequate—God's grace is enough! God's power is made perfect in your weakness. You can become all God has called you to be.

As parents, **when we remember our calling and that our children are gifts God has entrusted to us, our approach to raising our children becomes more God-centered**. In moments of frustration or disobedience, we can pause, look at our children, and marvel at the person God is shaping each one to be.

Delight in who they are. Ask God to help you see them as people who are created in God's image and being formed by God's Spirit, and let that be the starting point for your guidance and correction.

We *partner* with God to raise children who carry God's love into the world.

Take the next small, faithful step—God's grace will meet you there.

"The one who calls you is faithful, and he will do it."
(1 Thessalonians 5:24)

Reflection

1. Do you resist change—finding it hard to step away from devices, social media, or gaming?

2. How do you feel about leading your family and modeling your values through everyday faith? What steps can you take to nurture supportive, values-aligned relationships around you?

3. Name three to five positive changes you've seen in your family since you began this journey. How can you affirm and thank your family for their efforts to build connection and peace?

4. Identify one area where your children can lead—at home and among peers. How will you support them as they practice everyday faith?

5. What do you believe God is calling you to as a parent, and where are you noticing His work in your family right now?

Family Conversation Starters

- "When did we feel peace and connection at home this week? What new habits bring us joy?"
- "When do we feel hurried most days? How can we slow down to practice patience and presence?"
- "What enjoyable activities have we done in place of screen time? What new ideas can we try next to grow joy and strengthen connection?"

Rhythms for This Week

1. Confess to God any resistance to the changes He's inviting you to make—so you can live faithfully and lead your family well. Pray for humility and grace to communicate change

to your family with a gentleness that fosters peace and connection.

2. Search your heart for regret over past failures. Ask for God's forgiveness and grace to start fresh.

3. Spend time reading the Bible—start a routine of journaling the verses or words that stir your heart. Set aside time every day to seek God's wisdom and guidance.

4. Make a wholehearted commitment to a values-based family life; what specific sacrifice will you embrace to make everyday faith real?

Bonus

HOMESCHOOLING BY FAITH

Reflections on what we've learned

ARE YOU CONSIDERING homeschooling? I'd love to share my reflections from our family's homeschooling journey with you.

Taking the lead role in your child's education can feel intimidating, but be encouraged: there are many excellent resources for homeschooling families and local and online communities to connect with that make the experience both doable and deeply rewarding.

With God's help, you can build everyday rhythms of learning at home that allow your family to thrive.

How did your homeschooling journey begin?

Soon after Willow turned two, friends began asking whether I'd registered her for the best local schools. When I mumbled that I planned to homeschool, the response was usually skepticism—and with every conversation, my insecurities grew.

Then one mom said something startling: "You can do it." As we talked, she helped me see that I was already homeschooling. "How did Willow learn to talk? Who taught her to walk? How is she learning to count and sing her ABCs?" She was right—I had already taught my daughter so much.

From then on, my answer changed: "I am a homeschool mom."

In that sense, all parents are homeschoolers. I started teaching Willow as a baby—just like every parent does—and I simply kept going.

Can you homeschool without a teaching degree?

Confession: I was terrified to begin formal homeschooling. Even though I'm a university professor who loves teaching, I felt inadequate when it came to teaching my own daughter. Looking back, I see why it felt so daunting. It's easy to believe homeschooling requires special credentials or complicated methods. Our systems are built around conventional schooling, and parents can feel ill-equipped.

There's no need to feel inadequate. For most of history, education happened at home or in small community settings with limited resources. When America was founded, many children were taught by their parents, often with rigorous expectations and strong literacy. Families didn't have the advanced, readily accessible curricula we enjoy today—yet children usually learned to read early—sometimes by reading Scripture with a parent, even the King James Version with its *thee*s and *thou*s.

It sounded unrealistic to me—and remarkable. I was willing to try. After meeting my friend, homeschool advocate Sam Sorbo, I felt free to create my own "curriculum." Willow was only three, so we simply explored God's beautiful world together. I built a rhythm of walks, time in nature, and learning from whatever we encountered. I hoped the rest would fall into place.

It did. By age five, Willow was reading the Bible independently. What surprised me most was that focusing on nature and enjoying life together didn't set her back academically—it inspired her to learn. With minimal screen time, she grew curious about words and began sounding them out on her own.

If you're considering homeschooling—or just taking a more active role in your child's education—you don't have to be intimidated. Lean on community: family and friends, local homeschool co-ops, church programs, online groups and resources, and the public library. God calls us to pass on truth to our children, and where God calls, He equips.

How can we start homeschooling in the early years?

Start with reading. Once children master basic reading skills, they can complete work independently and enjoy activity books on their own, and daily life gets simpler for you. As independence grows, you can tidy the kitchen, answer emails, or reorganize a closet while they work nearby and ask questions as needed. Reading and writing also provide meaningful daytime "busywork": cards to write, books to enjoy, activity pages to finish—and later, a few carefully chosen educational apps.

Teaching a child to read can feel intimidating. Here's what worked for us. Larry taught Willow letters and sounds when she was two; by three, she was sounding out basic words like "stop." At four, I introduced the Bob Books series—we kept it fun and laughed at the silly pictures. Once she had the basic sounds, we practiced with simple books and neighborhood signs.

At five, Willow built literacy with Explode the Code, a traditional phonics program that teaches the patterns of English rather than relying on memorization of sight words. As she recognized those patterns, she could sound out almost any word. The remaining task was vocabulary, which my husband and I reinforced naturally in daily life.

For curriculum, try one program; if it doesn't fit, switch for the next subject and try a different program. Invite your child's input. Offer a few subjects and see what interests them. It's natural for children to become engrossed in a topic; we often focus on one subject for a month, completing a year's curriculum in that window. Each month, we explored a different subject of her choice.

In homeschooling, you can set the pace and catch up easily. Our routine is to do schoolwork every day except Sunday. That hour or so of study starts my day well—a quick tidying of the house, meal planning, then catching up on emails. For Willow, it gives structure and predictability. It puts her in a learning mindset, and after schoolwork she's more likely to choose something constructive than ask for screen time. Since we include schoolwork on Saturdays, during the summer, and over holidays, we can take days off any time.

(For a discussion on helping kids focus—without power struggles—see chapter 6.)

What challenges have you faced in homeschooling?

Being home most days means Willow sometimes gets bored. Planning activities can feel like a hassle, but it's part of our reality. I invest in quality supplies for her hobbies and often tell her to create something.

We get lonely, too. Staying connected takes intentionality. Playdates and video calls are helpful, and we've been blessed to meet several homeschooling families through our church. That little circle has made a big difference.

When we're unsure about curriculum, we ask other homeschool parents what worked for them. Families often share resources. Learning also happens outside the home—co-ops, extracurriculars, and free programs at the library or recreation center. We also visit the library for a change of pace.

Homeschooling can strain a family's finances. We've found creative solutions, and we're blessed to be able to work from home. But we've sacrificed to make it possible.

For me, the biggest challenge is the emotional investment. Answering questions, making decisions, and disciplining all day can be draining. I'm used to the constant companionship; I love being with Willow, yet sometimes I want a few minutes to myself—and when I finally get them, I miss her.

The challenges remain, but for us, the benefits far outweigh them because we see how faith, family, and learning weave together and help Willow thrive.

What has surprised you with joy?

Here are our favorite aspects of homeschooling.

Our **schedule is flexible** and adapts to fun opportunities as they arise. We aren't rushed. With one-on-one attention, Willow finishes core work quickly, leaving long stretches for hobbies and practical skills—cooking, baking, cleaning, gardening, laundry—and for simple acts of kindness. We can vacation or host weekday guests without derailing our routine. (And I'm grateful I don't have to pack a lunch every day.)

Educationally, it's a blessing to **monitor content**. We discuss her studies through the lens of our values and experiences. We review work on the spot so errors don't stick, and we talk through answers that differ from the textbook—often her reasoning is valid. That affirmation encourages independent thinking.

Homeschooling lets us tailor learning to Willow's **personality, learning style, and interests**, which makes school a joy. I set the semester's subjects; she chooses the order and how many to tackle at once. When she was young, we emphasized reading. Now she prefers two or three subjects a day. If frustration rises, we stop and try again tomorrow—or switch subjects for a week or two and let the new material sink in.

We also shape study time around how she learns best. She loves to move, and movement boosts her focus. When she was little, she did lessons in a wagon on our walks; now she often completes assignments while we're driving. At home, she might stand and stretch or lie on her bed to read. We'll add music, take short breaks, or study outside.

One-on-one teaching lets me **respond to emotions** in real time. If a lesson is hard, we reduce the number of pages; if it's easy, we do more.

We keep the mood light and loving—pausing to laugh, joke, share a hug, play a quick game, or grab a fun snack.

Homeschooling **strengthens our relationship**. We spend our days together, having meaningful conversations and making memories. I have a front-row seat to watch her grow, and I can affirm and guide her at each step. I get to be present for the spark of understanding and help as soon as she needs it.

When I asked Willow why she likes homeschooling, she said: "I get to play all day, except for a few minutes, and be with my mom." I'm glad she sees creative learning and free time as play.

Most of all, homeschooling lets us grow together in faith and love.

Continue your journey with this award-winning study

Women in the Bible

BY MARINA HOFMAN

Discover the courage, faith, and perseverance of women whose
stories reveal God's strength in everyday life—
and be inspired to live boldly in your own.

CASTLE QUAY BOOKS

.